150 EXTRA-EASY
ORNAMENTS
IN PLASTIC CANVAS

It's fun — and easy — to fashion your own ornaments with this creative Christmas craft book. You'll find over 150 plastic canvas decorations to trim your tree, from traditional holiday favorites such as Santas, snowmen, and angels to nostalgic quilt blocks, birdhouses, and more. There are even some ornaments that double as party favors and package trims, along with two tree toppers. Adding a personalized look to your Christmas celebration has never been easier!

LEISURE ARTS, INC.
and
OXMOOR HOUSE, INC.

LEISURE ARTS PRESENTS
150 EXTRA-EASY ORNAMENTS IN PLASTIC CANVAS

EDITORIAL STAFF

Vice President and Editor-in-Chief:
Anne Van Wagner Childs
Executive Director: Sandra Graham Case
Editorial Director: Susan Frantz Wiles
Publications Director: Carla Bentley
Creative Art Director: Gloria Bearden
Senior Graphics Art Director: Melinda Stout

PRODUCTION
Senior Publications Editor: Sherry Taylor O'Connor
Managing Editor: Lisa Truxton Curton
Senior Editor: Catherine Hubmann
Senior Project Coordinator: Charlotte Loftin
Project Coordinator: Susan McManus Johnson
Project Assistants: Alice Crowder, JoAnn Forrest, and
Judd Mann

DESIGN
Design Director: Patricia Wallenfang Sowers

EDITORIAL
Managing Editor: Linda L. Trimble
Associate Editor: Darla Burdette Kelsay
Assistant Editors: Tammi Williamson Bradley,
Terri Leming Davidson, and Robyn Sheffield-Edwards
Copy Editor: Laura Lee Weland

ART
Graphics Art Director: Rhonda Hodge Shelby
Senior Production Artist: Katie Murphy
Production Artists: Sonya McFatrich,
Brent Miller, Dana Vaughn, Mary Ellen Wilhelm,
Karen L. Wilson, and Dianna K. Winters
Photography Stylists: Pamela Perrymore Choate,
Laura Dell, Aurora Huston, and Courtney Frazier Jones

BUSINESS STAFF

Publisher: Bruce Akin
Vice President, Marketing: Guy A. Crossley
Marketing Manager: Byron L. Taylor
Print Production Manager: Laura Lockhart
Vice President and General Manager: Thomas L. Carlisle
Retail Sales Director: Richard Tignor

Vice President, Retail Marketing: Pam Stebbins
Retail Marketing Director: Margaret Sweetin
Retail Customer Service Manager: Carolyn Pruss
General Merchandise Manager: Russ Barnett
Vice President, Finance: Tom Siebenmorgen
Distribution Director: Ed M. Strackbein

150 EXTRA-EASY ORNAMENTS IN PLASTIC CANVAS
from the *Plastic Canvas Creations* series
Published by Leisure Arts, Inc., and Oxmoor House, Inc.

Library of Congress Catalog Number 96-78951
Hardcover ISBN 0-8487-1582-9
Softcover ISBN 1-57486-044-5

TABLE OF CONTENTS

WOODLAND WONDERS 4

SANTA BASKET 9

CHARMING ANGELS.................10

SANTA & HIS ELVES 12

WINTER STARS 14

STOCKINGS GALORE 16

SHIMMERING SHAPES.................20

ENCHANTING VILLAGE 22

WHITE CHRISTMAS 24

GLAD TIDINGS 28

HOLY FAMILY 29

NOSTALGIC QUILT BLOCKS............32

MERRY MINI BASKETS 34

SANTA TREE TOPPER 35

SNOW FAMILY 38

NOAH AND COMPANY 40

FESTIVE PHRASES 44

GINGERBREAD HOUSE 46

BEADED SNOWFLAKE 48

BAND OF ANGELS 49

CUTE AS A BUTTON 52

SIMPLE NATIVITY.....................54

CHRISTMAS CANDLE 56

SCRIPTURE SAMPLERS 57

MR. & MRS. SNOWMAN 60

OLD-TIME CAROLERS 62

WINSOME MEDLEY 64

LOVABLE SANTA.......................69

CLASSROOM FAVORITES..............70

BABY'S FIRST CHRISTMAS 72

HOLIDAY BIRDHOUSES 73

POTPOURRI CUBES 76

CANDY CANE FRAME 78

LACY TREETOP ANGEL 79

FESTIVE PETS 82

MOOD MESSAGES 84

NORTH POLE TRIO.......................85

SANTA STAR 90

TEDDY POINSETTIA 91

GENERAL INSTRUCTIONS 92

Woodland Wonders

Featuring silhouettes of woodland scenes and wildlife, this rustic set evokes images of the snowy North Woods. Miniature log carriers, an evergreen, and a snowflake reflect the outdoor spirit. Cozy-looking mitten and stocking ornaments add warmth.

WOODLAND WONDERS

Stitches Used: Gobelin Stitch, Mosaic Stitch, Overcast Stitch, Smyrna Cross Stitch, and Tent Stitch

Christmas Tree Size: 3¹/₂"w x 3³/₄"h
Christmas Tree Supplies: Worsted weight yarn, clear 7 mesh plastic canvas, #16 tapestry needle, 4mm red wooden beads, sewing needle, and nylon thread
Christmas Tree Instructions: Follow charts to cut and stitch pieces. Use sewing needle and nylon thread to attach beads to both sides of pieces. Slide Side A into Side B. Tack top of Side A to top of Side B.

Christmas Tree design by Elaine Golden.

Snowflake Size: 3¹/₂"w x 3¹/₂"h
Snowflake Supplies: Worsted weight yarn, clear 7 mesh plastic canvas, and #16 tapestry needle
Snowflake Instructions: Follow chart to cut and stitch ornament.

Diamond Size: 4³/₄"w x 4³/₄"h each
Diamond Supplies: Worsted weight yarn, ivory 7 mesh plastic canvas, and #16 tapestry needle
Diamond Instructions: Follow chart to cut and stitch desired ornament.

Stocking Size: 2¹/₄"w x 4¹/₄"h
Stocking Supplies: Worsted weight yarn, clear 7 mesh plastic canvas, and #16 tapestry needle
Stocking Instructions: Follow charts to cut and stitch pieces. Referring to photo for color overcast stitches used, join Side A to Side B. Refer to General Instructions, page 96, to make a 3" red and black yarn twist. Tack yarn twist to ornament for hanger.

Snowflake (24 x 24 threads)
Cover edges with
ecru overcast stitches.

Christmas Tree Side A
(24 x 25 threads)
Cover edges with matching
color overcast stitches.

Christmas Tree Side B
(24 x 24 threads)
Cover edges with matching
color overcast stitches.

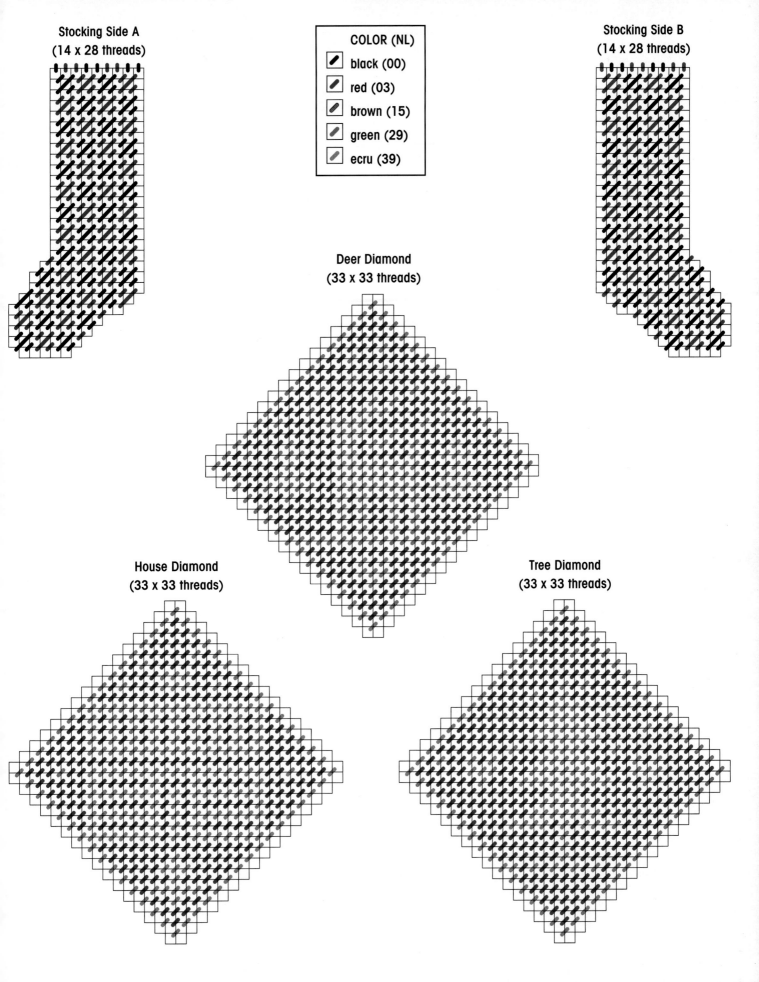

Stocking Side A
(14 x 28 threads)

Stocking Side B
(14 x 28 threads)

COLOR (NL)

- black (00)
- red (03)
- brown (15)
- green (29)
- ecru (39)

Deer Diamond
(33 x 33 threads)

House Diamond
(33 x 33 threads)

Tree Diamond
(33 x 33 threads)

Mittens Size: 2¼"w x 3"h each

Mittens Supplies: Worsted weight yarn, clear 7 mesh plastic canvas, and #16 tapestry needle

Mittens Instructions: Follow charts to cut and stitch pieces. With wrong sides together, use matching color overcast stitches to join one Mitten Side A to one Mitten Side B. Repeat for remaining Mitten Sides. Refer to General Instructions, page 96, to make a 4½" red and ecru yarn twist. Tack yarn twist between Mittens.

Mittens design by Janet Pomeroy.

COLOR (NL)	
red (03)	
ecru (39)	

Mitten Side A
(21 x 20 threads)
(Stitch 2)

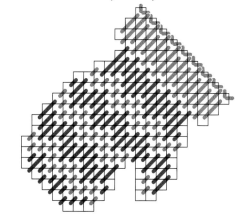

Mitten Side B
(21 x 20 threads)
(Stitch 2)

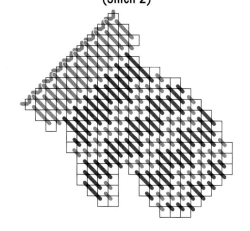

Mini Log Carrier Size: 2¼"w x 2½"h x 1½"d each

Mini Log Carrier Supplies: Sport weight yarn, ivory 10 mesh plastic canvas, #20 tapestry needle, sewing needle, nylon thread, twigs, and clear-drying craft glue

Mini Log Carrier Instructions: Follow chart to cut and stitch desired ornament. Use nylon thread to tack short edges together. Using yarn to match backstitches along edges of ornament, refer to General Instructions on page 96 to make a 4" yarn twist. Tack yarn twist to ornament for handle. Glue several twigs inside Carrier.

Tree Mini Log Carrier
(29 x 62 threads)

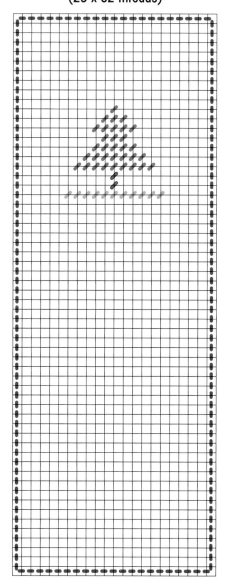

Poinsettia Mini Log Carrier
(29 x 62 threads)

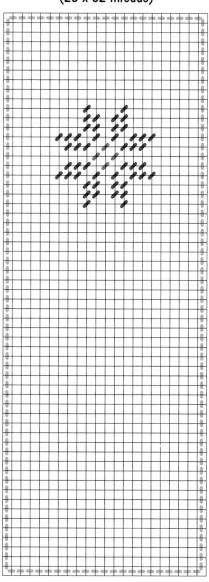

COLOR	
red	
brown	
gold	
green	

SANTA BASKET

Size: 3¹/₄"w x 5"h x 2"d

Supplies: Worsted weight yarn, 7 mesh plastic canvas, #16 tapestry needle, and clear-drying craft glue

Stitches Used: Backstitch, French Knot, Gobelin Stitch, Overcast Stitch, and Tent Stitch

Instructions: Follow charts to cut and stitch pieces, leaving stitches in shaded area unworked. Matching ★'s, complete stitches in shaded areas to join Handle to Front and Back. Join Front and Back along unworked edges. Glue Holly to Front and Back.

Santa Basket design by Dick Martin.

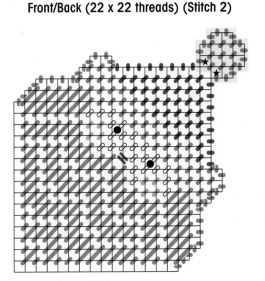

Santa Basket

This little Santa basket not only makes a cute ornament for your tree, but it also doubles as a whimsical party favor. Just tuck a sweet treat inside as a token of holiday cheer!

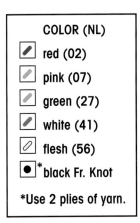

COLOR (NL)	
⬛	red (02)
⬛	pink (07)
⬛	green (27)
⬛	white (41)
⬜	flesh (56)
⬤*	black Fr. Knot

*Use 2 plies of yarn.

**Holly
(10 x 8 threads)
(Stitch 2)**

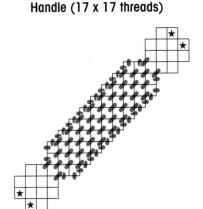

Handle (17 x 17 threads)

Front/Back (22 x 22 threads) (Stitch 2)

Charming Angels

Colorful flowers give these little angels the charm of a Dutch garden in bloom. Stitched on 10 mesh plastic canvas, the sweet trio is accented with metallic gold braid and embroidery floss.

CHARMING ANGELS

Size: 2"w x 3½"h each

Supplies: Sport weight yarn, embroidery floss, metallic gold braid, 10 mesh plastic canvas, and #20 tapestry needle

Stitches Used: Cross Stitch, French Knot, Overcast Stitch, and Tent Stitch

Instructions: Follow chart to cut and stitch desired ornament. Referring to photo for color overcast stitches used, cover unworked edges.

Charming Angels designs by Maryanne Moreck.

Angel A (21 x 34 threads)

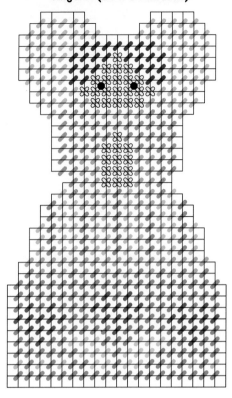

YARN

▱	white
▱	red
▱	pink
▱	lt green
▱	dk green
▱	gold
▱	lt gold

FLOSS

▱	*flesh
●	†black Fr. Knot

*Use twelve strands.

†Use six strands.

BRAID

▱	gold

Angel B (21 x 34 threads)

Angel C (21 x 34 threads)

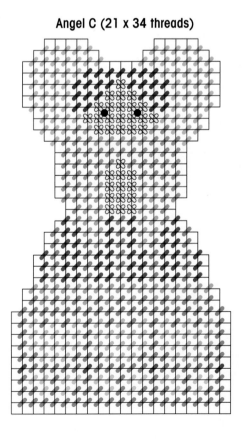

Santa & His Elves

This whimsical Santa and his playful companions offer a fun way to ring in the season. The colorful string of Christmas "lights" will be a bright addition to your tree, too!

SANTA & HIS ELVES
Stitches Used: Cross Stitch, French Knot, Gobelin Stitch, Overcast Stitch, and Tent Stitch

Elf A Size: 4"w x 5½"h
Elf A Supplies: Worsted weight yarn, clear 7 mesh plastic canvas, white 7 mesh plastic canvas, #16 tapestry needle, and 8" of thin gold cord
Elf A Instructions: Follow chart to cut and stitch Elf A on clear canvas. Cut one Snowflake from white canvas. Thread Snowflake onto gold cord and tack cord to Elf's hand.

Elf B Size: 4"w x 7"h
Elf B Supplies: Worsted weight yarn, clear 7 mesh plastic canvas, white 7 mesh plastic canvas, #16 tapestry needle, 12" of gold covered wire, and clear-drying craft glue
Elf B Instructions: Follow chart to cut and stitch Elf B on clear canvas. Cut five Snowflakes from white canvas. Coil gold wire around a pencil. Slide wire off pencil and gently stretch wire into loose curve shape. Thread ends of wire through Elf's hands and twist to secure. Glue Snowflakes to wire.

Santa Size: 2¾"w x 6¾"h
Santa Supplies: Worsted weight yarn, clear 7 mesh plastic canvas, #16 tapestry needle, 7mm red pom-pom, 6" of ¼"w white satin ribbon, ¾" gold jingle bell, and clear-drying craft glue
Santa Instructions: Follow chart to cut and stitch Santa. Glue pom-pom to Santa. Thread white ribbon through jingle bell. Glue ends of ribbon to wrong side of Santa.

Light Size: 1¼"w x 2"h each

Light Supplies: Worsted weight yarn, clear 7 mesh plastic canvas, #16 tapestry needle, ⅛"w black satin ribbon, sewing needle, and black sewing thread

Light Instructions: Follow charts to cut and stitch Light pieces. Join pieces. Use sewing needle and thread to tack Light to ribbon. Spacing Lights 6" apart, repeat for desired number of Lights.

Light
(9 x 14 threads)
(Stitch 2 for each Light)

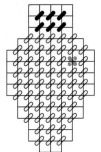

Elf A (33 x 33 threads)
Cover remaining unworked edges
with matching color overcast stitches.

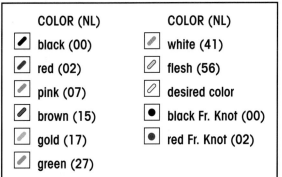

COLOR (NL)	COLOR (NL)
black (00)	white (41)
red (02)	flesh (56)
pink (07)	desired color
brown (15)	● black Fr. Knot (00)
gold (17)	● red Fr. Knot (02)
green (27)	

Snowflake
(4 x 4 threads)

Santa (32 x 32 threads)
Cover unworked edges with
matching color overcast stitches.

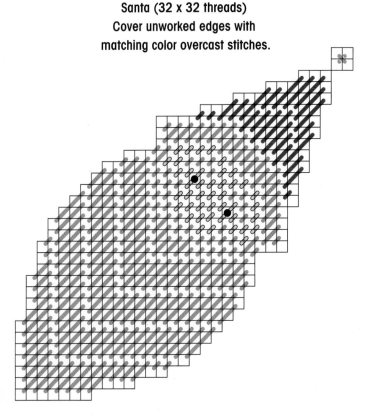

Elf B (33 x 33 threads)
Cover remaining unworked edges
with matching color overcast stitches.

Winter Stars

Sparkling clear and bright, these Christmas stars are reminiscent of a winter night. The geometric patterns are stitched in icy blue and white on precut canvas stars to reflect a frosty glow.

WINTER STARS

Star A Size: 5¹⁄₂"w x 5¹⁄₂"h

Star B, C, or D Size: 4"w x 4"h each

Supplies: Worsted weight yarn, Uniek® 5" plastic canvas star shape, and #16 tapestry needle

Stitches Used: Backstitch, Gobelin Stitch, Overcast Stitch, and Tent Stitch

Instructions: For Star B, C, or D, cut three threads from outside edge of canvas star shape. Follow chart to stitch desired Star. Cover unworked edges with blue overcast stitches.

Winter Stars designs by Ann Townsend.

COLOR (NL)	
	blue (35)
	lt blue (36)
	white (41)
	cutting line

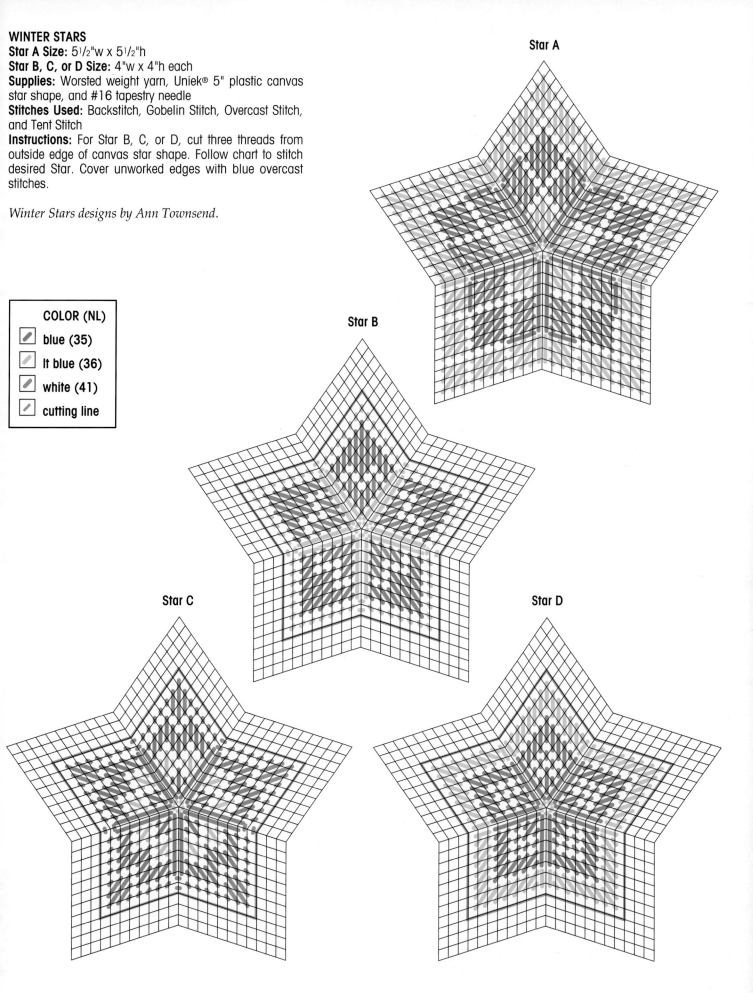

Star A

Star B

Star C

Star D

Stockings Galore

This merry assortment of miniature stockings features a host of holiday motifs reflecting the spirit of Christmas. From snowmen and reindeer to cheerful messages, the collection offers designs the whole family will enjoy!

STOCKINGS GALORE

Size: 2"w x 3¹/₄"h x ¹/₂"d each

Supplies: Sport weight yarn, metallic gold yarn, 10 mesh plastic canvas, #20 tapestry needle, ¹/₈"w satin ribbon, and clear-drying craft glue

Stitches Used: Backstitch, Cross Stitch, Double Cross Stitch, French Knot, Overcast Stitch, Tent Stitch, and Upright Cross Stitch

Instructions: Follow chart to cut and stitch desired Front. Numbers chart may be used to add year. Cut and stitch Side and matching Back. Join Front and Back to Side. Thread 6" of ribbon through Side at ★ to form a loop hanger. Knot ribbon ends on wrong side to secure hanger.

For Peace Stocking: Glue a ribbon bow to Front.

Stockings Galore designs by Nancy Dorman.

COLOR
▨ desired color

Side
(6 x 75 threads)

Back A (20 x 32 threads)
Matches Joy, Noel, Reindeer,
Santa, Teddy, or Wreath Front.

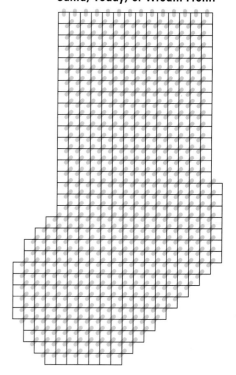

Back B (20 x 32 threads)
Matches Candle, Cardinal,
Poinsettia, or Snowman Front.

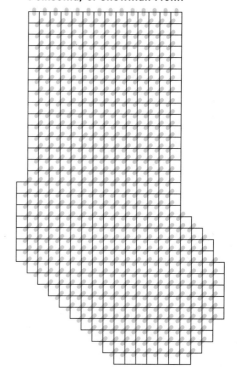

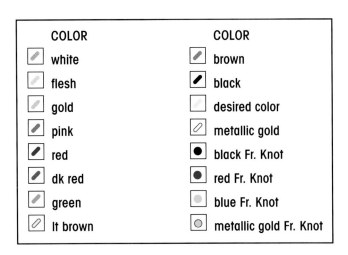

COLOR		COLOR	
white		brown	
flesh		black	
gold		desired color	
pink		metallic gold	
red		black Fr. Knot	
dk red		red Fr. Knot	
green		blue Fr. Knot	
lt brown		metallic gold Fr. Knot	

Poinsettia Front (20 x 32 threads)

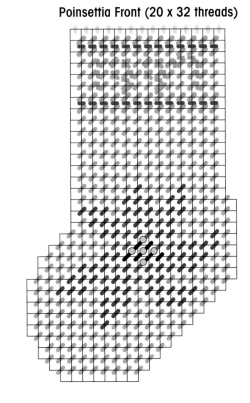

Numbers

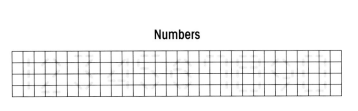

Wreath Front (20 x 32 threads)

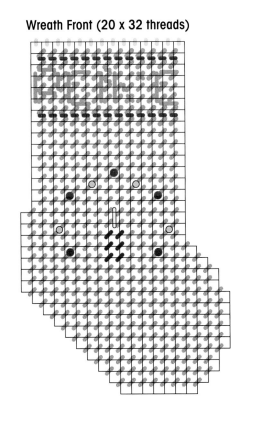

Santa Front (20 x 32 threads)

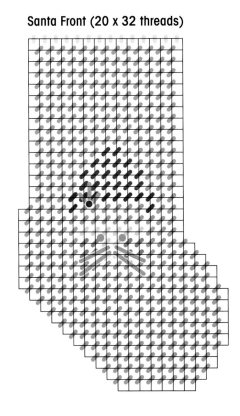

Teddy Front (20 x 32 threads)

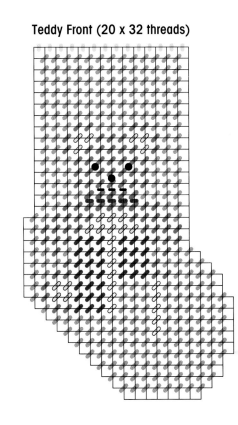

Snowman Front (20 x 32 threads)

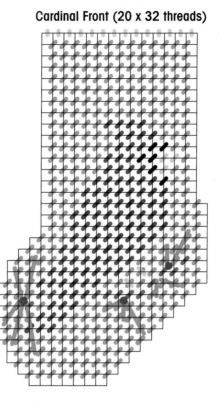

Cardinal Front (20 x 32 threads)

Candle Front (20 x 32 threads)

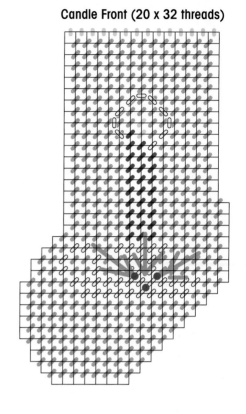

Noel Front (20 x 32 threads)

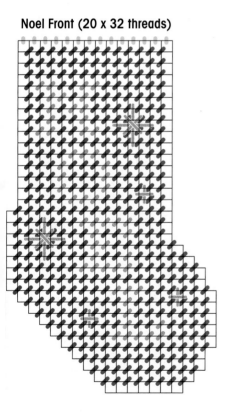

Joy Front (20 x 32 threads)

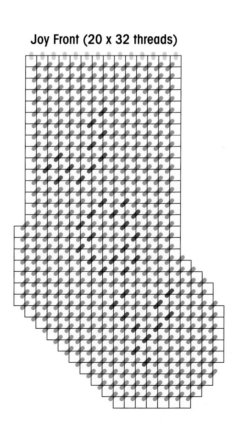

Reindeer Front (20 x 32 threads)

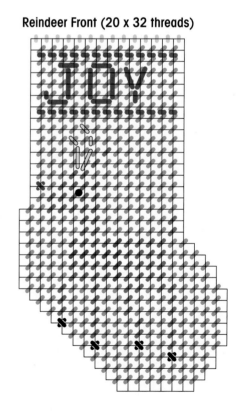

SHIMMERING SHAPES

Inspired by the exquisite handcrafted glass ornaments of Germany, these shimmering adornments offer a grand way to decorate the evergreen. The set includes five spectacular shapes.

SHIMMERING SHAPES

Approx. Size: 2³/₄"w x 3¹/₂"h x 2³/₄"d each

Supplies: Worsted weight yarn, metallic gold yarn, 7 mesh plastic canvas, and #16 tapestry needle

Stitches Used: Backstitch, Gobelin Stitch, Overcast Stitch, and Tent Stitch

Instructions: Follow chart to cut and stitch pieces for desired ornament. Referring to photo for color overcast stitches used, join two pieces along one side between ✳'s and ▲'s. Matching ✳'s and ▲'s, join edges of third piece to unworked edges of first two pieces.

Shimmering Shapes designs by Celia Lange.

	COLOR (NL)
⬦	red (02)
⬦	dk red (03)
⬦	green (27)
⬦	white (41)
⬦	metallic gold

Heart (24 x 25 threads) (Stitch 3)

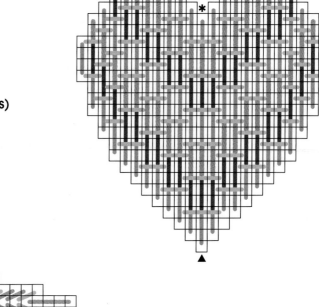

**Star
(22 x 28 threads)
(Stitch 3)**

**Diamond A
(14 x 26 threads)
(Stitch 3)**

**Bell
(22 x 22 threads)
(Stitch 3)**

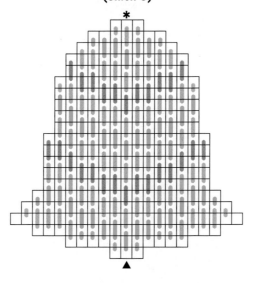

**Diamond B
(16 x 22 threads)
(Stitch 3)**

Enchanting Village

These quaint little ornaments call to mind cozy cottages decked in Christmas finery. The trio can be stitched in a variety of color schemes to create an enchanting village for your tree.

ENCHANTING VILLAGE

Approx. Size: 3"w x 3½"h each

Supplies: Worsted weight yarn, 7 mesh plastic canvas, #16 tapestry needle, and clear-drying craft glue

Stitches Used: Alternating Overcast Stitch, Backstitch, Cross Stitch, French Knot, Gobelin Stitch, Lazy Daisy Stitch, Overcast Stitch, and Tent Stitch

Instructions: Follow chart(s) to cut and stitch piece(s) for desired ornament. Glue pieces together.

Enchanting Village designs by Kooler Design Studio.

HOUSE A

COLOR (NL)	COLOR
▨ brown (14)	◉ *red Fr. Knot
▨ yellow (19)	● *gold Fr. Knot
▨ white (41)	◉ *blue Fr. Knot
▨ lt green (51)	◉ *green Fr. Knot
▨ *white	⬭ *green Lazy Daisy
▨ *red	*Use 2 plies of yarn.
▨ *green	

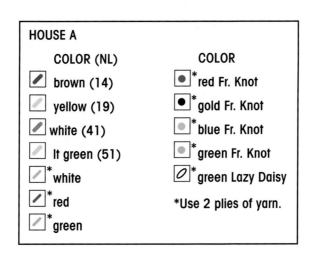

House A (19 x 22 threads)

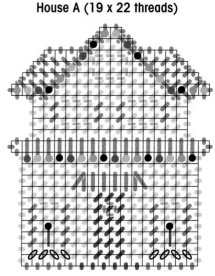

HOUSE B

COLOR (NL)	COLOR
▨ yellow (19)	▨ *red
▨ green (27)	▨ *dk blue
▨ dk blue (33)	● *red Fr. Knot
▨ lt blue (34)	● *gold Fr. Knot
▨ grey (38)	◉ *blue Fr. Knot
▨ white (41)	◉ *green Fr. Knot
▨ *white	*Use 2 plies of yarn.

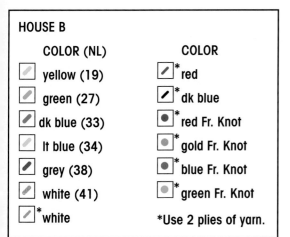

House B Front
(10 x 19 threads)

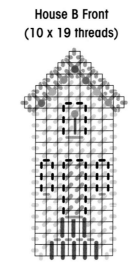

House B (22 x 19 threads)

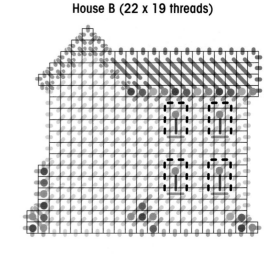

HOUSE C

COLOR	COLOR
▨ red (01)	▨ dk grey
▨ brown (14)	▨ *red
▨ dk brown (15)	▨ *dk grey
▨ yellow (19)	● *red Fr. Knot
▨ green (27)	◉ *gold Fr. Knot
▨ grey (37)	*Use 2 plies of yarn.
▨ white (41)	

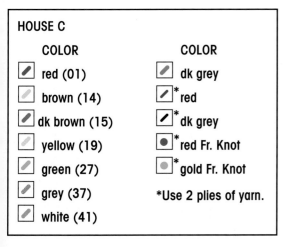

House C Chimney
(14 x 25 threads)

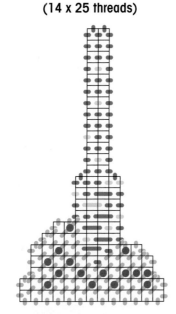

House C (22 x 24 threads)

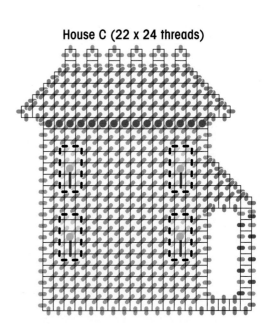

White Christmas

Set the stage for a white Christmas with this imaginative assortment! You'll find traditional holiday symbols such as a dove of peace and a star, along with more playful ornaments like our Christmas cat and mouse.

24

WHITE CHRISTMAS

Approx. Size: 3½"w x 3½"h each
Supplies: Worsted weight yarn, 7 mesh plastic canvas, #16 tapestry needle, and clear-drying craft glue
Additional Supplies for Bear, Cat, Tree, or Wreath: 10" of ¼"w red satin ribbon
Stitches Used: Backstitch, Cross Stitch, French Knot, Gobelin Stitch, Mosaic Stitch, Overcast Stitch, Scotch Stitch, Tent Stitch, and Upright Cross Stitch
Instructions: Follow chart(s) to cut and stitch piece (s) for desired ornament. Use matching color overcast stitches to cover unworked edges.
For Bear, Cat, Tree, or Wreath: Tie ribbon into a bow and glue in place.
For Horn: Glue Holly to Horn.
For Mouse Tail: Thread 8" of white yarn to right side of ornament at ▲. Referring to photo, use white yarn to tack tail in place.

White Christmas designs by Dick Martin.

COLOR (NL)	
✎	black (00)
✎	red (02)
✎	pink (07)
✎	gold (11)
✎	green (27)
✎	white (41)
●	black Fr. Knot (00)
●	red Fr. Knot (02)
●	green Fr. Knot (27)

Cat (23 x 34 threads)

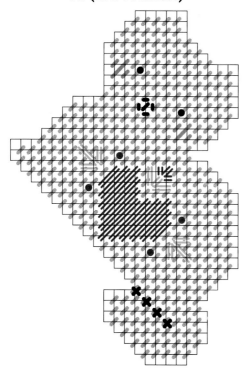

Star (26 x 26 threads)

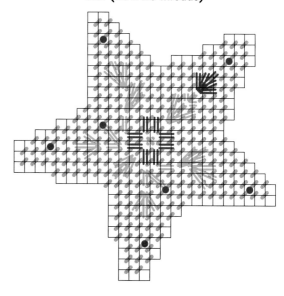

Tree (25 x 25 threads)

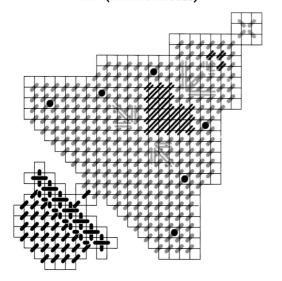

Candle (25 x 25 threads)

Mouse (22 x 24 threads)

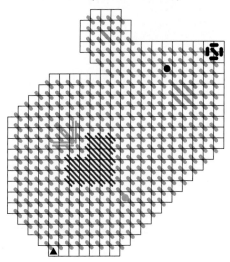

Wreath (22 x 22 threads)

**Horn Holly
(8 x 8 threads)**

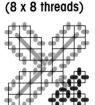

Horn (27 x 27 threads)

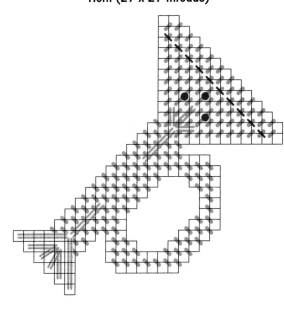

Candy Cane (29 x 22 threads)

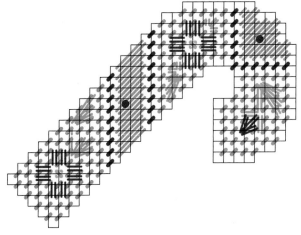

Dove (24 x 25 threads)

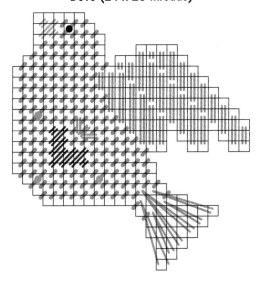

Bear (27 x 27 threads)

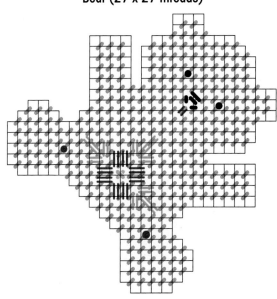

Glad Tidings

These ornaments proclaim glad tidings of "Peace," "Love," and "Joy." For variety, we used a different color scheme for each motif, but you can also stitch them in the same shade for a uniform look.

GLAD TIDINGS

Size: 4³/₄"w x 4¹/₂"h each

Supplies: Worsted weight yarn, metallic gold yarn, 7 mesh plastic canvas, and #16 tapestry needle

Stitches Used: Backstitch, Cross Stitch, Gobelin Stitch, Overcast Stitch, and Tent Stitch

Instructions: Follow chart to cut and stitch ornament. Add desired word to area outlined in green. Referring to photo for color overcast stitches used, cover unworked edges.

Glad Tidings designs by MizFitz.

Ornament (32 x 31 threads)

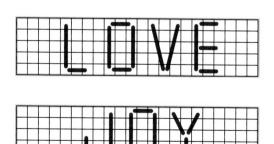

COLOR

✎	desired color
✎	white
✎	metallic gold

Holy Family

Worked on 14 mesh plastic canvas using embroidery floss, this divine set features Mary, Joseph, and Baby Jesus. The exquisite ornaments are sure to become cherished heirlooms.

HOLY FAMILY

Baby Jesus Size: 1½"w x 2¼"h
Mary Size: 1¾"w x 3¾"h
Joseph Size: 2"w x 4¼"h
Supplies: Embroidery floss, Kreinik metallic gold (002) #8 fine braid, ivory 14 mesh plastic canvas, and #24 tapestry needle
Stitches Used: Backstitch, French Knot, and Tent Stitch
Instructions: Follow chart to cut and stitch desired ornament. Use six strands of floss unless otherwise indicated in color key.

Holy Family designs by Maryanne Moreck.

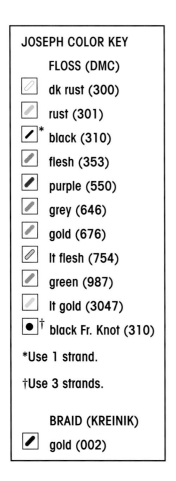

JOSEPH COLOR KEY

FLOSS (DMC)

⊘	dk rust (300)
⊘	rust (301)
⟋*	black (310)
⟋	flesh (353)
⟋	purple (550)
⟋	grey (646)
⟋	gold (676)
⊘	lt flesh (754)
⟋	green (987)
⟋	lt gold (3047)
●†	black Fr. Knot (310)

*Use 1 strand.

†Use 3 strands.

BRAID (KREINIK)

⟋	gold (002)

Joseph (30 x 58 threads)

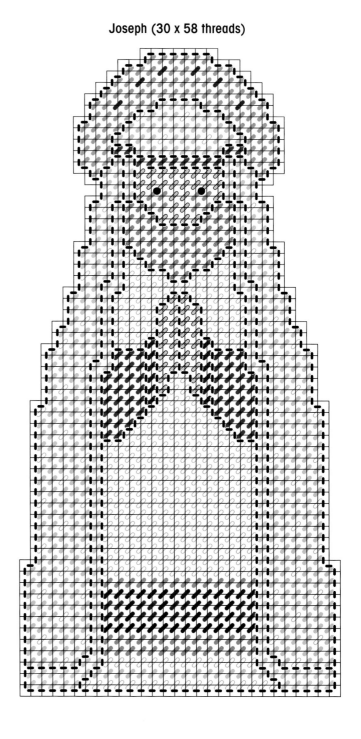

30

MARY COLOR KEY

FLOSS (DMC)	FLOSS (DMC)
✏*black (310)	✏ lt gold (3047)
✏ blue (322)	✏ rose (3733)
✏ dk blue (336)	●† black Fr. Knot (310)
✏ flesh (353)	*Use 1 strand.
✏ red (498)	†Use 3 strands.
✏ gold (676)	
✏ ecru (712)	BRAID (KREINIK)
✏ lt flesh (754)	✏ gold (002)
✏ lt brown (869)	

BABY JESUS COLOR KEY

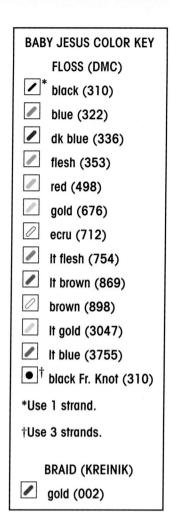

FLOSS (DMC)

✏* black (310)

✏ blue (322)

✏ dk blue (336)

✏ flesh (353)

✏ red (498)

✏ gold (676)

✏ ecru (712)

✏ lt flesh (754)

✏ lt brown (869)

✏ brown (898)

✏ lt gold (3047)

✏ lt blue (3755)

●† black Fr. Knot (310)

*Use 1 strand.

†Use 3 strands.

BRAID (KREINIK)

✏ gold (002)

Mary (25 x 53 threads)

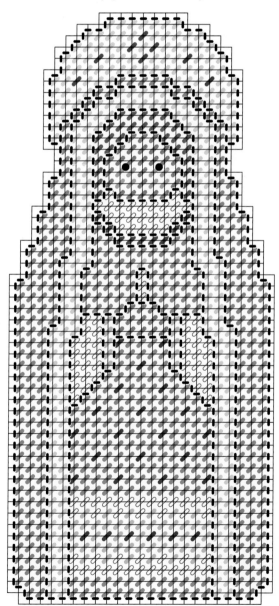

Baby Jesus (23 x 31 threads)

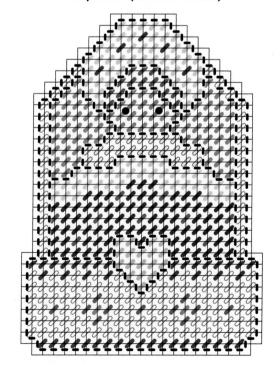

31

Nostalgic Quilt Blocks

Use these miniature quilt block ornaments to create a charming "patchwork" tree. Stitched in soft colors, the familiar patterns bring to mind images of gentler days.

NOSTALGIC QUILT BLOCKS

Size: 2"w x 2"h each
Supplies: Worsted weight yarn, 7 mesh plastic canvas, #16 tapestry needle, and polyester fiberfill
Stitches Used: Gobelin Stitch, Mosaic Stitch, Overcast Stitch, Scotch Stitch, and Tent Stitch
Instructions: Follow chart to cut and stitch pieces for desired ornament. Join pieces, lightly stuffing ornament with fiberfill before joining is completed.

Nostalgic Quilt Blocks designs by Mary Billeaudeau.

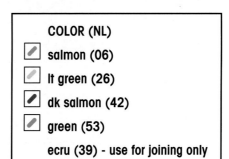

COLOR (NL)

▱	salmon (06)
▱	lt green (26)
▰	dk salmon (42)
▰	green (53)
	ecru (39) - use for joining only

Front/Back (14 x 14 threads each) (Stitch 2 matching pieces)

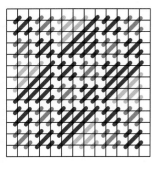

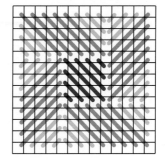
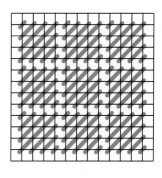

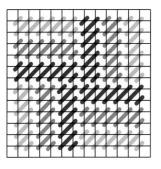
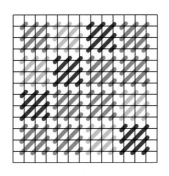
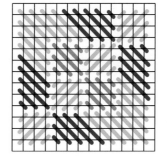
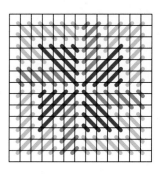

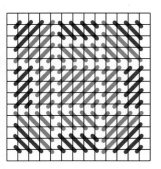
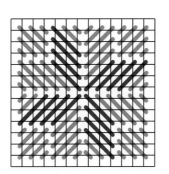

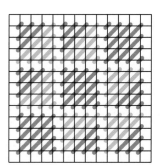

Merry Mini Baskets

Filled with colorful candy or festive holiday greenery, these merry miniatures make magical ornaments. The trio is quick and easy to make, even for beginners!

MERRY MINI BASKETS

Size: 2½"w x 3"h x 1¾"d each

Supplies: Worsted weight yarn, 7 mesh plastic canvas, #16 tapestry needle, and clear-drying craft glue

Additional Holly Basket Supplies: Three red ¼" pom-poms

Stitches Used: Backstitch, Cross Stitch, French Knot, Gobelin Stitch, Overcast Stitch, and Tent Stitch

Instructions: Follow charts to cut and stitch Basket pieces and desired Motif piece(s). Join Sides to Front/Back. Join Bottom to Front/Back and Sides. Glue Motif to Basket.

For Holly Basket: Glue pom-poms to basket.

Holly Basket design by Studio M.

COLOR (NL)	
✎	red (02)
✎	green (27)
✎	white (41)
✎	flesh (56)
✎	desired color
●*	black Fr. Knot

*Use 2 plies of yarn.

Basket Front/Back
(16 x 45 threads)

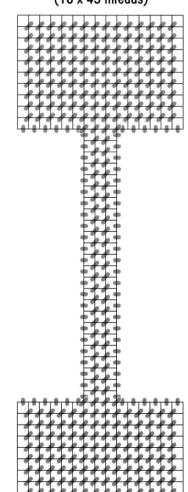

Wreath Motif
(11 x 11 threads)

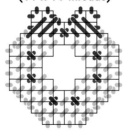

Santa Motif
(10 x 10 threads)

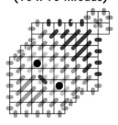

Leaf Motif
(9 x 6 threads)
(Stitch 3)

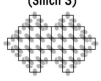

Basket Bottom
(16 x 11 threads)

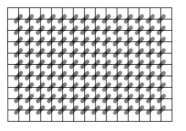

Basket Side
(11 x 11 threads)
(Stitch 2)

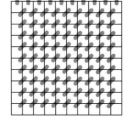

Santa Tree Topper

This Santa tree topper will not only bring joy to your Christmas tree, but it will also serve as a reminder for little ones that the jolly old elf is watching to see who's been naughty or nice!

SANTA TREE TOPPER

Size: 7½"w x 9¾"h

Supplies: Worsted weight yarn, three 10½" x 13½" sheets of 7 mesh plastic canvas, and #16 tapestry needle

Stitches Used: Backstitch, Cross Stitch, Gobelin Stitch, Overcast Stitch, and Tent Stitch

Instructions: Follow charts to cut and stitch pieces. Tack Holly and Small Leaf to Hat Brim. Match long unworked edges of Face and Hat Brim to unworked thread of Front and join by stitching through all thicknesses of canvas. Join Front and Hat Brim to Back along remaining unworked edges.

Santa Tree Topper design by Dick Martin.

Hat Brim (40 x 10 threads)

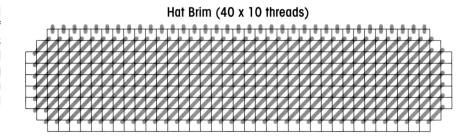

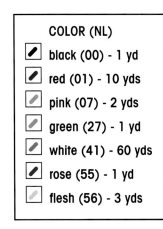

Front (50 x 55 threads)

Face (50 x 32 threads)

Back (50 x 55 threads)

Holly (9 x 9 threads)

Small Leaf (7 x 7 threads)

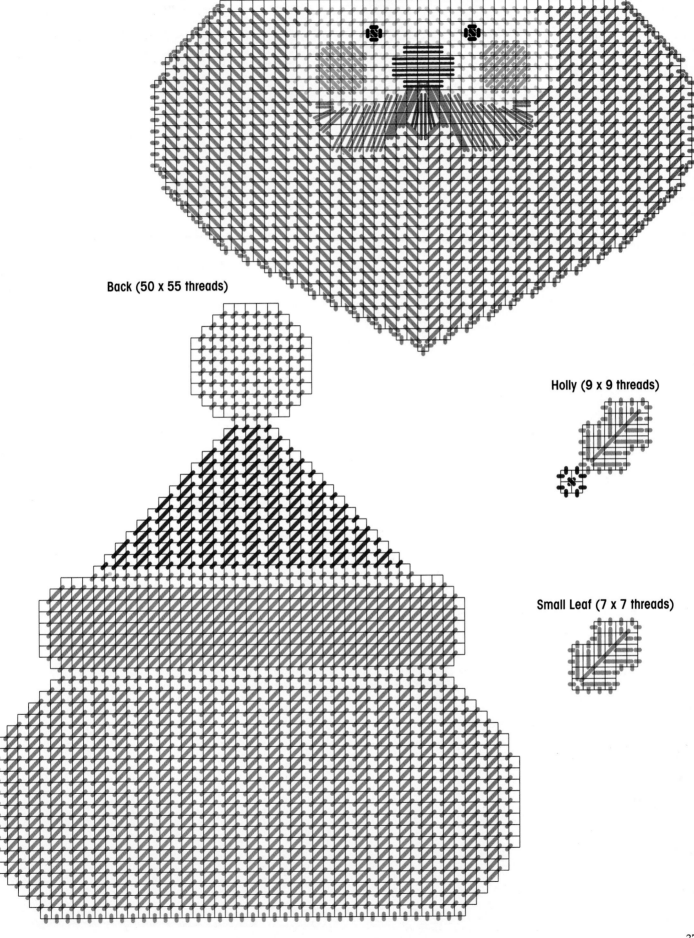

Snow Family

We couldn't stop with just one snowman — we created a whole frosty family! We topped Mom and Dad with cozy caps and outfitted the entire crew with braided mufflers. French knots provide the "lumps of coal" for their eyes and buttons, and snowflakes add to the wintry fun.

SNOW FAMILY

Approx. Size: 2¹/₂"w x 4"h each

Supplies: Worsted weight yarn, embroidery floss, 7 mesh plastic canvas, #16 tapestry needle, and clear-drying craft glue

Stitches Used: Backstitch, Double Cross Stitch, French Knot, Gobelin Stitch, Lazy Daisy Stitch, Overcast Stitch, and Tent Stitch

Instructions: Follow charts to cut and stitch pieces for desired ornament. Use matching color overcast stitches to cover unworked edges. Glue pieces together. For scarf, braid desired color yarn and trim to desired length. Tie scarf around ornament.

Snow Family designs by Becky Dill.

YARN (NL)
✎ black (00)
✎ red (02)
✎ brown (14)
✎ white (41)

FLOSS (DMC)
✎ pink (335)
✎ green (699)
● black Fr. Knot (310)
● orange Fr. Knot (947)
⬭ green Lazy Daisy (699)

Child's Arm
(10 x 4 threads) (Stitch 2)

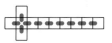

Child (10 x 20 threads)

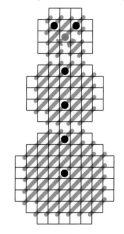

Snowflake (14 x 14 threads)

Mama's/Papa's Left Arm
(9 x 9 threads)

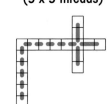

Mama's/Papa's Right Arm
(9 x 9 threads)

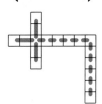

Papa's Hat (8 x 6 threads)

Baby (6 x 8 threads)

Mama's Hat (8 x 5 threads)

Papa (14 x 32 threads)

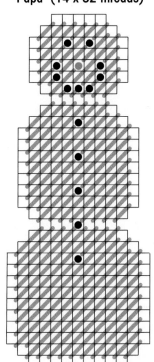

Toddler's Arm
(7 x 4 threads) (Stitch 2)

Toddler (8 x 17 threads)

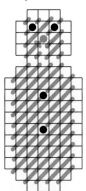

Mama (12 x 29 threads)

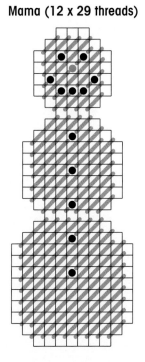

Noah and Company

You won't miss the boat with this delightful crew illuminating your evergreen! Complete with a rainbow that reminds us of God's mercy and His faithfulness to His word, Noah and company beautifully portray the timeless Bible story.

NOAH AND COMPANY

Approx. Size: 2½"w x 2½"h each
Supplies: Worsted weight yarn, 7 mesh plastic canvas, and #16 tapestry needle
Stitches Used: Backstitch, French Knot, Gobelin Stitch, Overcast Stitch, and Tent Stitch
Instructions: Follow chart to cut and stitch desired ornament.
For Noah's belt: Thread 10" of tan yarn through ornament at ▲'s, leaving loose ends extending from front of ornament. Tie yarn ends into a knot and trim ends to ½" long.

For Elephant's tail: Thread 6" of grey yarn through stitches on wrong side of ornament, leaving yarn end extending from ornament at ★. Trim end to ¾" long.
For Giraffe's tail: Thread 6" of yellow yarn through stitches on wrong side of ornament, leaving yarn end extending from ornament at ■. Trim end to ¾" long.
For Zebra's tail: Cut three 8" lengths of white yarn and one 8" length of black yarn. Knot two white lengths and black length together close to one end. Thread needle with loose ends of yarn. Thread needle through stitches on wrong side of Zebra,

leaving loose ends extending from Zebra at ✦. Braid loose ends to 1" long and tie remaining length of white yarn into a knot around end of braid to secure. Trim ends to ¼" and separate into plies.

Ark, Giraffe, and Rainbow designs by Becky Dill.
Noah, Alligator, Dove, Elephant, Flamingo, Monkey, Pig, Tiger, and Zebra designs by Dick Martin.

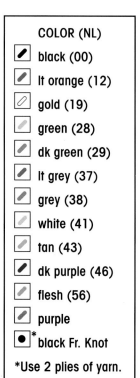

COLOR (NL)

- black (00)
- lt orange (12)
- gold (19)
- green (28)
- dk green (29)
- lt grey (37)
- grey (38)
- white (41)
- tan (43)
- dk purple (46)
- flesh (56)
- purple
- ● * black Fr. Knot

*Use 2 plies of yarn.

Alligator (28 x 6 threads)

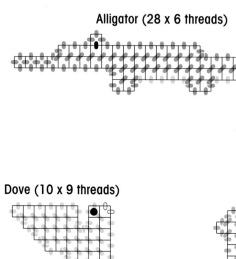

Dove (10 x 9 threads)

Pig (15 x 14 threads)

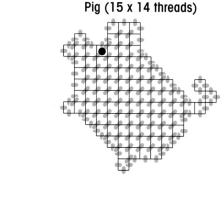

Tiger (18 x 20 threads)

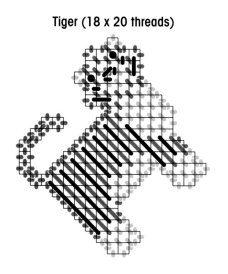

Elephant (16 x 19 threads)

Noah (14 x 20 threads)

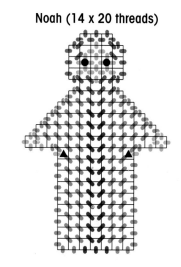

42

COLOR (NL)

- black (00)
- red (01)
- pink (07)
- brown (14)
- green (29)
- blue (33)
- grey (38)
- white (41)
- tan (43)
- dk purple (46)
- orange (52)
- yellow (57)
- ● *black Fr. Knot

*Use 2 plies of yarn.

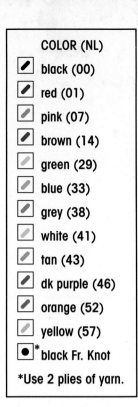

Rainbow (30 x 18 threads)

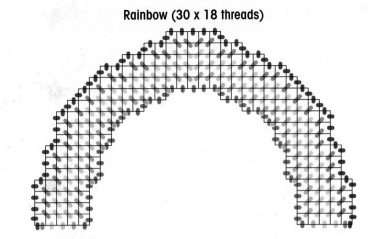

Ark (34 x 22 threads)

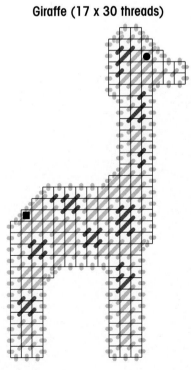

Monkey (13 x 22 threads)

Giraffe (17 x 30 threads)

Flamingo (13 x 21 threads)

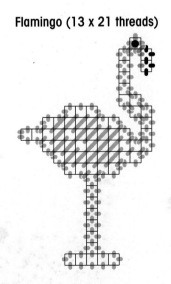

Zebra (14 x 19 threads)

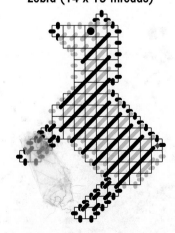

43

Festive Phrases

Here's a clever way to spread holiday cheer — hang these happy holiday messages on the tree! The festive phrases also make great Christmas decor or you can use them as pretty package finishes.

FESTIVE PHRASES

Joy Size: 4¹/₂"w x 1³/₄"h
Noel Size: 6"w x 1³/₄"h
Ho Ho Ho Size: 2³/₄"w x 5¹/₂"h
Supplies: Worsted weight yarn, 7 mesh plastic canvas, #16 tapestry needle, and clear-drying craft glue
Additional Joy Supplies: 10" of ¹/₄"w red satin ribbon and five 7mm red pom-poms
Additional Noel Supplies: Three 7mm red pom-poms
Additional Ho Ho Ho Supplies: Three 10" lengths of ¹/₄"w red satin ribbon
Stitches Used: Overcast Stitch and Tent Stitch
Instructions: Follow chart(s) to cut and stitch piece(s) for desired ornament.
For Joy: Tie ribbon into a bow. Glue bow and pom-poms to ornament.
For Noel: Glue Holly and pom-poms to ornament.
For Ho Ho Ho: Tie ribbon into bows and glue to ornament.

Festive Phrases designs by Studio M.

COLOR (NL)	
✎	red (02)
✎	green (27)

Holly
(6 x 4 threads)
(Stitch 5)

HO HO HO (19 x 36 threads)

JOY (30 x 12 threads)

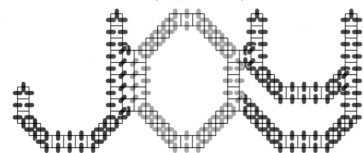

NOEL (40 x 12 threads)

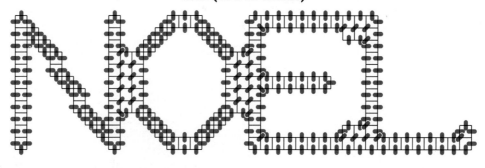

Gingerbread House

Embellished with faux candy canes, gumdrops, and lollipops, this sweet little gingerbread house pays tribute to the earliest Christmas trees, which were trimmed almost entirely with edible ornaments.

GINGERBREAD HOUSE

Size: 3³/₄"w x 3¹/₂"h x 3"d
Supplies: Worsted weight yarn, 7 mesh plastic canvas, #16 tapestry needle, and clear-drying craft glue
Stitches Used: Backstitch, French Knot, Gobelin Stitch, Overcast Stitch, and Tent Stitch
Instructions: Follow charts to cut and stitch pieces. Use brown overcast stitches to join one long edge of each Eave to one long edge of each Side and to join Chimney pieces. For remaining steps, use white overcast stitches. Join short edges of Eaves and Sides to Front and Back. Join Front, Back, and Sides to Bottom. Join one unworked edge of each Roof piece to the unworked edge of each Eave. Join Roof pieces along remaining unworked edges. Tack top of Front and Back to Roof. Tack Chimney to Roof. Glue remaining pieces to House.

Gingerbread House design by Becky Dill.

COLOR (NL)	
	red (02)
	pink (07)
	brown (13)
	white (41)
	desired color
	* dk red
●	* black Fr. Knot
●	* pink Fr. Knot

*Use 2 plies of yarn.

Gumdrop
(4 x 4 threads)
(Stitch 5)

Peppermint
(5 x 5 threads)
(Stitch 2)

Gingerbread Man
(8 x 8 threads)

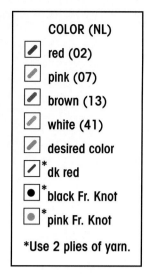

Chimney Side A
(4 x 4 threads)

Chimney Side B
(4 x 6 threads)

Door
(6 x 7 threads)

Lollipop (4 x 7 threads)
(Stitch 5)

Candy Cane A
(5 x 6 threads)
(Stitch 2)

Candy Cane B
(5 x 6 threads)
(Stitch 2)

Chimney Front
(4 x 6 threads)

Chimney Back
(4 x 6 threads)

Side (16 x 8 threads) (Stitch 2)

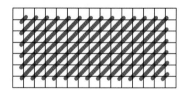

Eave (16 x 4 threads) (Stitch 2)

Trim A (17 x 4 threads) (Stitch 2)

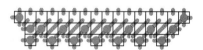

Trim B (17 x 4 threads) (Stitch 2)

Bottom (16 x 16 threads)

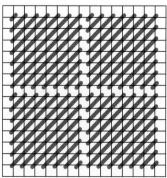

Front/Back (22 x 19 threads) (Stitch 2)

Roof (16 x 17 threads) (Stitch 2)

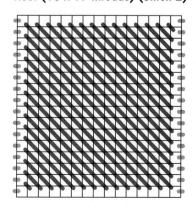

Beaded Snowflake

Uniquely beautiful, this snowflake embodies all the wonder of a white Christmas. Stitch a flurry of them for your tree, or enjoy the ornament alone as a reminder of its individuality. Pearl beads give the decoration its brilliance.

Side
(14 x 28 threads)
(Stitch 4)

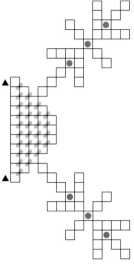

BEADED SNOWFLAKE

Size: 5³/₄"w x 5³/₄"h x 4¹/₂"d

Supplies: Worsted weight yarn, 7 mesh plastic canvas, #16 tapestry needle, 80 white 3mm pearl beads, beading needle, and nylon thread

Stitches Used: Overcast Stitch and Tent Stitch

Instructions: Follow charts to cut pieces and work tent stitches. Leaving edges between ▲'s unworked, cover unworked edges of all pieces with white overcast stitches. Use nylon thread and beading needle to attach beads to both sides of stitched pieces. With right sides together, join two Sides between ▲'s. Repeat with remaining Side sections. Matching ▲'s, place one set of Sides each on front and back of Center. Using nylon thread, stitch through all thicknesses to join Sides to Center.

Beaded Snowflake design by Vicki Blizzard.

Center (38 x 38 threads)

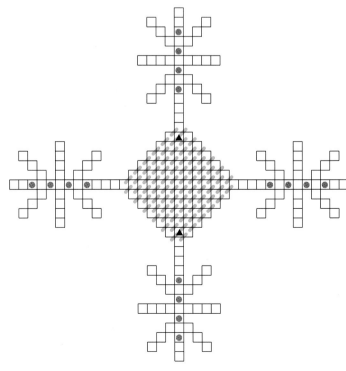

COLOR	
▨	white
◉	bead

48

Band of Angels

This heavenly quartet will inspire you to fill your home with the music of Christmas. The angelic ornaments make beautiful gifts, too.

BAND OF ANGELS

Harpist Size: 5³/₄"w x 5"h
Flutist Size: 4³/₄"w x 5¹/₄"h
Cellist Size: 4³/₄"w x 6¹/₄"h
Trumpeter Size: 5¹/₂"w x 7¹/₄"h
Supplies: Worsted weight yarn, metallic gold yarn, 7 mesh plastic canvas, and #16 tapestry needle
Additional Harpist Supplies: Kreinik metallic gold (002) #8 fine braid
Additional Flutist Supplies: Metallic silver yarn
Additional Cellist Supplies: Kreinik metallic gold (002) #8 fine braid and metallic silver yarn
Stitches Used: Backstitch, Gobelin Stitch, Overcast Stitch, and Tent Stitch
Instructions: Follow chart to cut and stitch desired ornament.

Band of Angels designs by Juliana Schiweck.

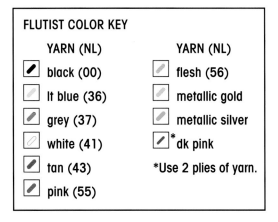

FLUTIST COLOR KEY

YARN (NL)	YARN (NL)
black (00)	flesh (56)
lt blue (36)	metallic gold
grey (37)	metallic silver
white (41)	*dk pink
tan (43)	*Use 2 plies of yarn.
pink (55)	

Flutist (32 x 35 threads)
Cover remaining unworked edges
with matching color overcast stitches.

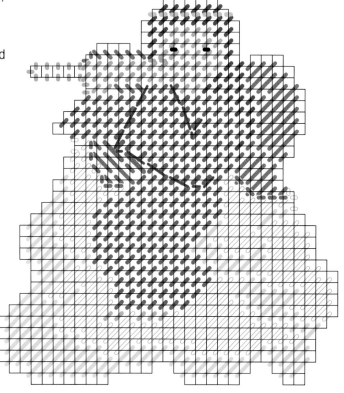

Harpist (39 x 34 threads)
Cover remaining unworked edges
with matching color overcast stitches.

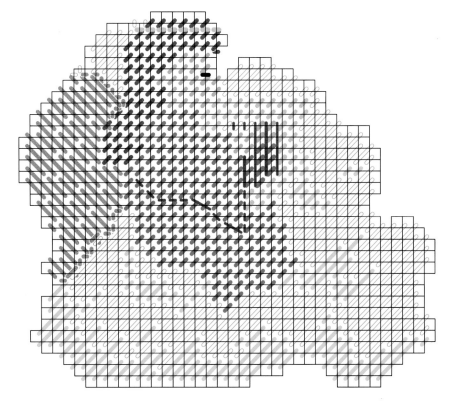

HARPIST COLOR KEY

YARN (NL)
black (00)
brown (14)
lt blue (36)
grey (37)
white (41)
purple (46)
flesh (56)
metallic gold
*dk purple
*Use 2 plies of yarn.

BRAID (KREINIK)

gold (002)

50

Cellist (32 x 42 threads)
Cover remaining unworked edges
with matching color overcast stitches.

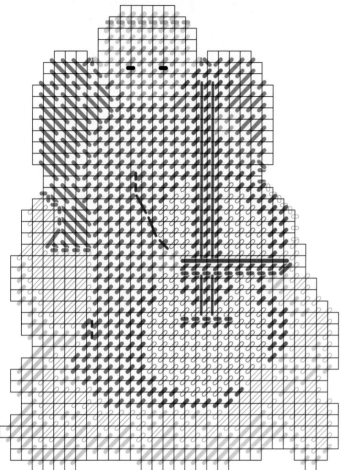

CELLIST COLOR KEY

	YARN (NL)		YARN (NL)
✏	black (00)	✏	flesh (56)
✏	brown (14)	✏	metallic gold
✏	dk brown (15)	✏	metallic silver
✏	dk blue (33)	✏*	dk blue
✏	blue (34)		*Use 2 plies of yarn.
✏	lt blue (36)		
✏	grey (37)		BRAID (KREINIK)
✏	white (41)	✏	gold (002)
✏	tan (43)		

Trumpeter (38 x 49 threads)
Cover remaining unworked edges
with matching color overcast stitches.

TRUMPETER COLOR KEY

YARN (NL)

✏	black (00)
✏	yellow (19)
✏	green (23)
✏	lt blue (36)
✏	grey (37)
✏	white (41)
✏	flesh (56)
✏	metallic gold
✏*	dk green

*Use 2 plies of yarn.

Cute As A Button

From the first snowflakes of winter to Santa's billowy beard, these colorful ornaments are bedecked with beads and buttons for added charm.

CUTE AS A BUTTON

Approx. Size: 4"w x 4"h each

Supplies: Worsted weight yarn, metallic gold yarn, 7 mesh plastic canvas, #16 tapestry needle, assorted beads and buttons, and clear-drying craft glue

Stitches Used: Backstitch, Cross Stitch, French Knot, Gobelin Stitch, Mosaic Stitch, Overcast Stitch, Scotch Stitch, and Tent Stitch

Instructions: Follow chart to cut and stitch desired ornament. Use matching color overcast stitches to cover unworked edges. Glue beads and buttons to ornament as desired.

COLOR (NL)	COLOR (NL)
black (00)	white (41)
red (02)	flesh (56)
pink (07)	metallic gold
brown (15)	pink Fr. Knot (07)
green (27)	

Bell (24 x 24 threads)

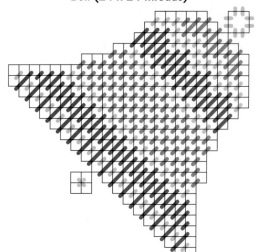

Wreath (25 x 25 threads)

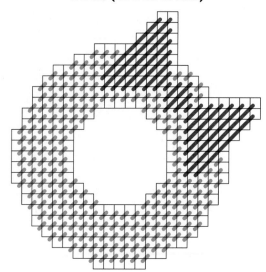

Snowflake (26 x 26 threads)

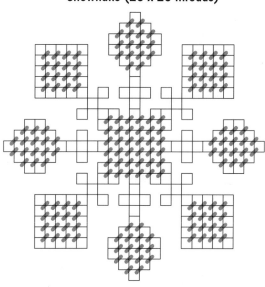

Tree (25 x 25 threads)

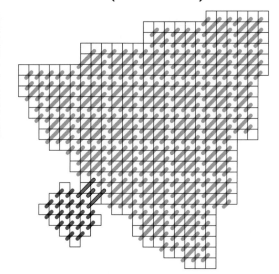

Santa (31 x 26 threads)

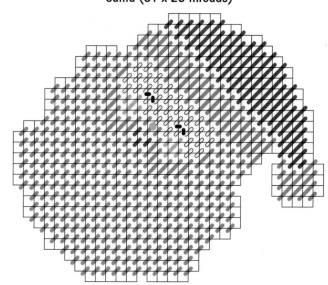

Simple Nativity

Designed to hang on your tree, this miniature Nativity scene is a touching reminder of the true reason for the season.

SIMPLE NATIVITY
Size: 4³/₄"w x 5"h
Supplies: Worsted weight yarn, Kreinik metallic gold (002) #8 medium braid, 7 mesh plastic canvas, #16 tapestry needle, and clear-drying craft glue
Stitches Used: Backstitch, French Knot, Gobelin Stitch, Overcast Stitch, Tent Stitch, Turkey Loop Stitch, and Turkey Loop Variation Stitch
Instructions: Follow charts to cut and stitch

pieces. For reins on each Camel: Secure 12" of brown yarn on wrong side of piece. Thread yarn to right side at ▲. Loop yarn around Camel's head and secure yarn on wrong side at ▲. For tail on each Camel: Tie a knot near one end of a 6" length of tan yarn. Thread needle with unknotted end of yarn. Secure yarn under stitches on wrong side of piece, leaving ³/₄" of knotted end extending at ★. For hay in Manger:

Turn Manger over. Thread 6" of lt yellow yarn under stitches near top edge on wrong side, leaving ends of yarn extending from each side of Manger. Trim ends to ¹/₄" long and separate into plies. Glue pieces to Stable in the following order: Joseph, Mary, Baby Jesus, Manger, Camel A, Camel B, Sheep A, Sheep B, and Star.

Simple Nativity design by Becky Dill.

54

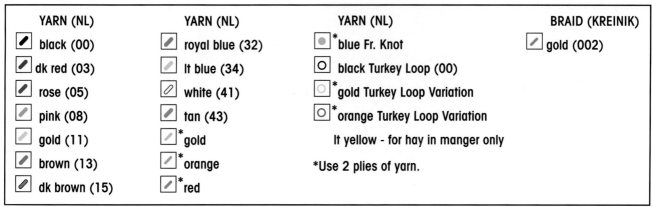

YARN (NL)

- ✏ black (00)
- ✏ dk red (03)
- ✏ rose (05)
- ✏ pink (08)
- ✏ gold (11)
- ✏ brown (13)
- ✏ dk brown (15)

YARN (NL)

- ✏ royal blue (32)
- ✏ lt blue (34)
- ✏ white (41)
- ✏ tan (43)
- ✏ *gold
- ✏ *orange
- ✏ *red

YARN (NL)

- ⦿ *blue Fr. Knot
- ⊙ black Turkey Loop (00)
- ⊙ *gold Turkey Loop Variation
- ⊙ *orange Turkey Loop Variation

  lt yellow - for hay in manger only

*Use 2 plies of yarn.

BRAID (KREINIK)

- ✏ gold (002)

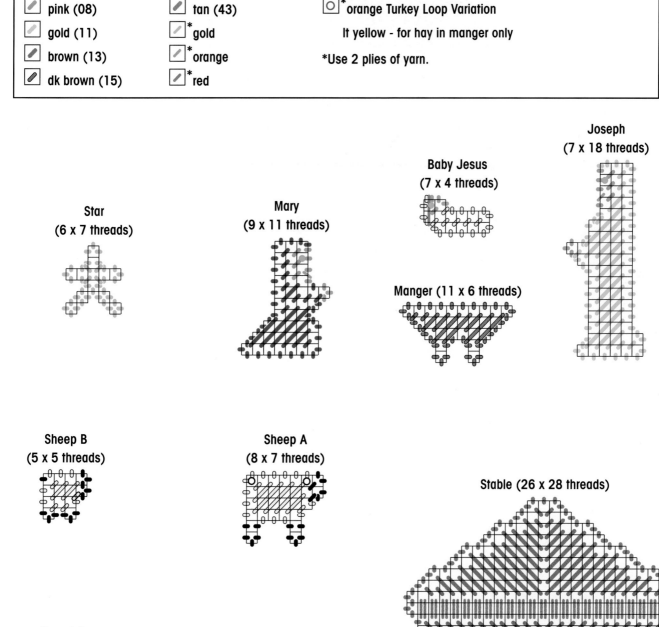

Star
(6 x 7 threads)

Mary
(9 x 11 threads)

Baby Jesus
(7 x 4 threads)

Joseph
(7 x 18 threads)

Manger (11 x 6 threads)

Sheep B
(5 x 5 threads)

Sheep A
(8 x 7 threads)

Stable (26 x 28 threads)

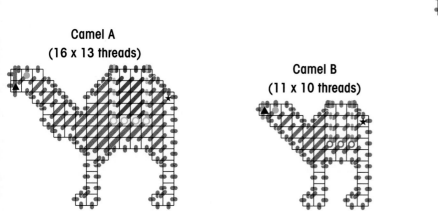

Camel A
(16 x 13 threads)

Camel B
(11 x 10 threads)

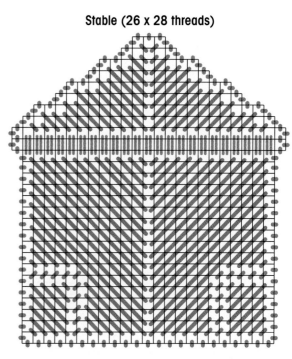

Christmas Candle

Our holiday candle recalls the tallow tapers that adorned Christmas trees of yesteryear. Worked using 7 mesh plastic canvas, the tree-trimmer is topped with a small light bulb — a "bright" idea for recycling those burned-out Christmas bulbs.

CHRISTMAS CANDLE

Size: 3³/₄"w x 4¹/₄"h x 3"d

Supplies: Worsted weight yarn, Kreinik metallic gold (002) #16 medium braid, 7 mesh plastic canvas, one 3" dia plastic canvas circle, #16 tapestry needle, three ¹/₂" red pom-poms, small light bulb, 6" of 6mm green chenille stem, and clear-drying craft glue

Stitches Used: Backstitch, Gobelin Stitch, Overcast Stitch, and Tent Stitch

Instructions: Follow charts to cut and stitch pieces. For fastener, fold chenille stem in half. Thread chenille stem over intersection at center of Base from right side to wrong side. Twist to secure. Join long edges of Candle, forming a cylinder. Join bottom edge of Candle to right side of Base. Join Rim along short edges, forming a circle. Join unworked edge of Rim to Base. Tack Handle to Rim. Glue Leaves and pom-poms to Candle. Glue light bulb into Candle. Use chenille stem to fasten ornament to tree.

Christmas Candle design by MizFitz.

YARN (NL)
- ⬛ red (02)
- ⬛ green (27)
- ⬛ ecru (39)

BRAID (KREINIK)
- ⬛ gold (002)

Base

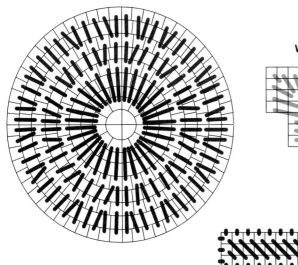

Leaves (19 x 10 threads)
Cover unworked edges
with green overcast stitches.

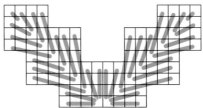

Handle (27 x 4 threads)

Candle (17 x 19 threads)

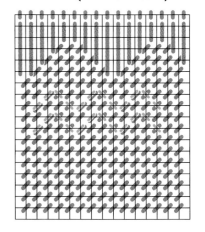

Rim (61 x 3 threads)

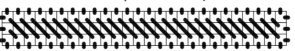

Scripture Samplers

These inspirational ornaments capture the enduring charm of old-fashioned samplers. The verses are stitched on 14 mesh plastic canvas using embroidery floss and displayed in bright 7 mesh frames.

SCRIPTURE SAMPLERS

Size: 3½"w x 3½"h each

Supplies: Worsted weight yarn, embroidery floss, Kreinik metallic gold (002) #16 medium braid, clear 7 mesh plastic canvas, white 14 mesh plastic canvas, #16 tapestry needle, and #24 tapestry needle

Stitches Used: Backstitch, Cross Stitch, French Knot, Gobelin Stitch, Overcast Stitch, and Tent Stitch

Instructions: Follow charts to cut and stitch Front, Back, and desired Insert. Use red floss to tack Insert behind opening in Front. Join Front to Back with worsted weight yarn overcast stitches.

Scripture Samplers designs by Ann Townsend.

COLOR	
◰	red (NL 01)
◰ *	red (DMC 321)
◰ *	green (DMC 699)
◰ *	blue (DMC 796)
● *	red Fr. Knot (DMC 321)
● †	blue Fr. Knot (DMC 796)
◰	gold (KREINIK 002) #16 braid

*Use 3 strands.

†Use 6 strands.

Front (25 x 25 threads)
Stitch on 7 mesh canvas
using #16 needle.

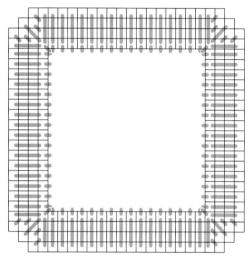

Back (25 x 25 threads)
Stitch on 7 mesh canvas
using #16 needle.

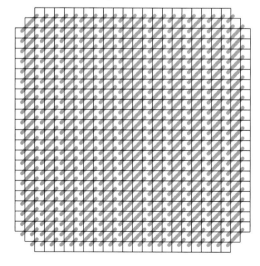

Insert (35 x 35 threads)
Stitch on white 14 mesh canvas
using #24 needle.

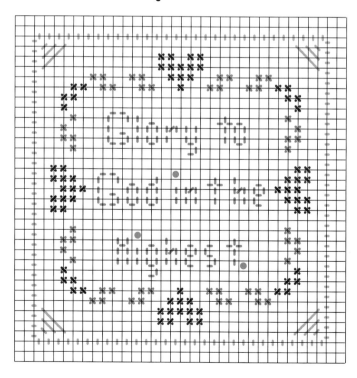

58

Inserts (35 x 35 threads each)
Stitch on white 14 mesh canvas using #24 needle.

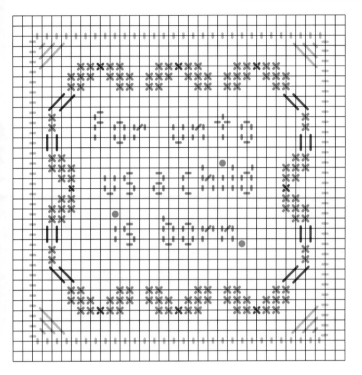

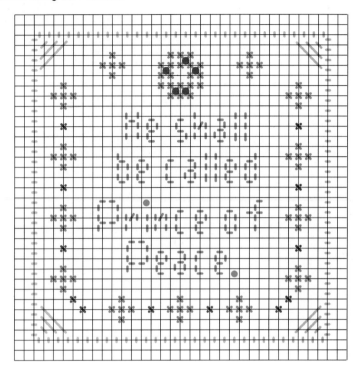

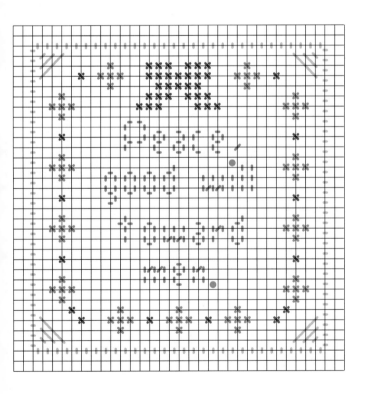

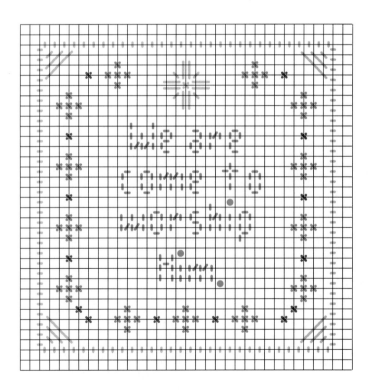

Mr. & Mrs. Snowman

Sporting colorful caps and French-knot smiles, this rosy-cheeked couple captures the wintry fun of making snowmen. The happy-go-lucky pair is sure to add cheer to your Christmas celebration.

MR. AND MRS. SNOWMAN

Mr. Snowman Size: 3½"w x 4¼"h x 1"d
Mrs. Snowman Size: 4½"w x 4¼"h x 1"d
Supplies: Worsted weight yarn, 7 mesh plastic canvas, and #16 tapestry needle
Additional Mrs. Snowman Supplies: 10" of ⅛"w blue satin ribbon and clear-drying craft glue
Stitches Used: Backstitch, Cross Stitch, French Knot, Gobelin Stitch, Overcast Stitch, and Tent Stitch
Instructions: Follow charts to cut and stitch pieces. Join Nose Side pieces. Referring to photo for color overcast stitches used, cover remaining unworked edges. Tack Nose in place.
For Mr. Snowman: Tack Holly to ornament.
For Mrs. Snowman: Tie ribbon into a bow and glue to ornament.

Mr. and Mrs. Snowman designs by Peggy Astle.

Mr. Snowman (24 x 28 threads)

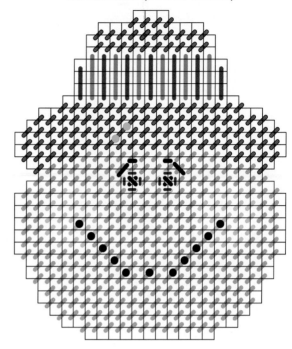

Nose Side
(6 x 6 threads)
(For Mr. Snowman, stitch 2)
(For Mrs. Snowman, stitch 2)

Holly
(8 x 6 threads)

Mrs. Snowman (30 x 28 threads)

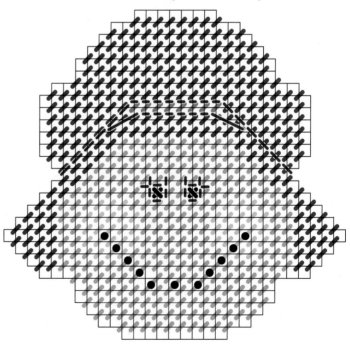

COLOR (NL)	
✏	black (00)
✏	red (02)
✏	pink (07)
✏	brown (13)
✏	green (27)
✏	blue (32)
✏	white (41)
✏	orange (52)
✏	*black
●	black Fr. Knot (00)
●	red Fr. Knot (02)

*Use 2 plies of yarn.

Old-Time Carolers

The tradition of caroling dates back to the first Christmas Eve, when the hills of Bethlehem echoed with angelic song. These joyful carolers honor the strolling singers who serenade us each year with their timeless Yuletide tunes.

OLD-TIME CAROLERS

Approx. Size: 2¹⁄₂"w x 5¹⁄₂"h each

Supplies: Worsted weight yarn, 7 mesh plastic canvas, #16 tapestry needle, and clear-drying craft glue

Stitches Used: Backstitch, French Knot, Gobelin Stitch, Lazy Daisy Stitch, Overcast Stitch, and Tent Stitch

Instructions: Follow charts to cut and stitch pieces for desired ornament, leaving shaded areas unworked. Turn piece over and stitch shaded areas on wrong side. Using matching color overcast stitches, cover unworked edges.

For Woman: Tack a white yarn bow to ornament at ★. Tack Songbook to hands.

For Man: Tack Songbook to hands. Glue Hat in place .

For Lamppost: Tack a red yarn bow to Wreath. Tack Wreath to Lamppost. Glue Lamppost to Snowdrift.

Old-Time Carolers designs by Becky Dill.

COLOR (NL)	
✎	black (00)
✎	red (02)
✎	brown (14)
▱	lt green (26)
▱	green (27)
▱	dk green (29)
▱	white (41)
▱	flesh (56)
✎	*red
✎	*green
●	black Fr. Knot (00)
●	brown Fr. Knot (14)
●	*white Fr. Knot
●	*red Fr. Knot
●	*gold Fr. Knot
◿	*yellow Lazy Daisy

*Use 2 plies of yarn.

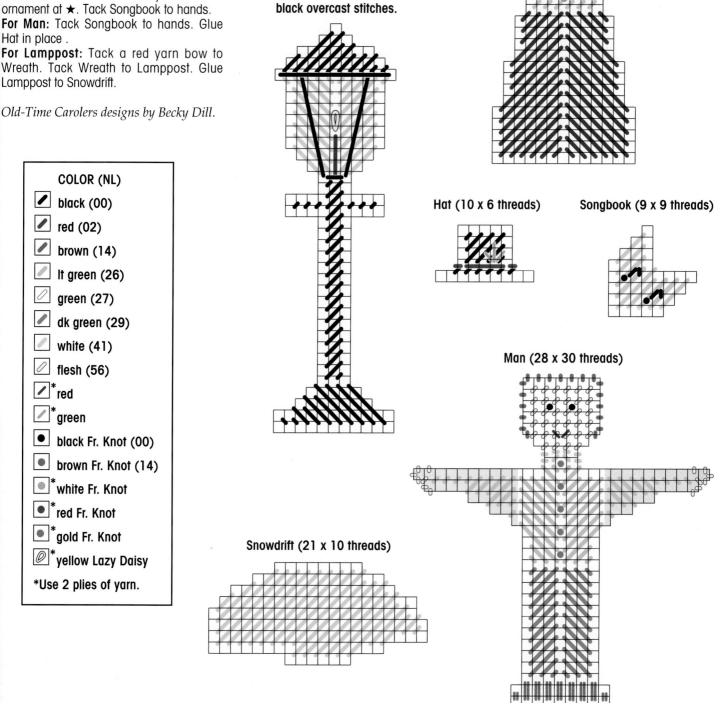

Wreath (6 x 6 threads)

Woman (28 x 31 threads)

Lamppost (12 x 37 threads)
Cover unworked edges with black overcast stitches.

Hat (10 x 6 threads)

Songbook (9 x 9 threads)

Man (28 x 30 threads)

Snowdrift (21 x 10 threads)

Winsome Medley

You'll find the Christmas images you love best in this cute collection — a playful snowman with real twig arms, a red-nosed reindeer, a jolly St. Nick, a sleigh loaded with presents, and lots more! All of these winsome ornaments are quick to make, too.

WINSOME MEDLEY

Approx. Size: 3½"w x 3½"h each

Supplies: Worsted weight yarn, 7 mesh plastic canvas, #16 tapestry needle, clear-drying craft glue and trim listed below

Sleigh Trim: Three 5mm red pom-poms and three desired color yarn bows

Santa Trim: Two 12mm moving eyes, one 7mm red pom-pom, one ¼" red pom-pom, and one ¾" white pom-pom

Reindeer Trim: Two 15mm moving eyes, two 5mm red pom-poms, one ½" red pom-pom, and 12" of black cloth-covered wire bent and trimmed for mouth

Snowman Trim: One 5mm red pom-pom, five 5mm black pom-poms, two 7mm black pom-poms, three 7mm yellow pom-poms, two small twigs, and 12" of ¼"w red satin ribbon tied into a bow

Tree Trim: Eleven 5mm red pom-poms

Joy Trim: Three 5mm red pom-poms

Stocking Trim: Three 5mm red pom-poms

Evergreen Trim: Two small pinecones and 12" of ¼"w red satin ribbon tied into a bow

Poinsettia Trim: Six 5mm red pom-poms and one 5mm yellow pom-pom

Stitches Used: Cross Stitch, French Knot, Fringe Stitch, Overcast Stitch, Smyrna Cross Stitch, and Tent Stitch

Instructions: Follow chart(s) to cut and stitch piece(s) for desired ornament. Use matching color overcast stitches to cover unworked edges. Glue pieces together and add trim.

Winsome Medley designs by Studio M.

COLOR (NL)

- black (00)
- red (02)
- dk pink (07)
- pink (08)
- gold (11)
- brown (15)
- green (27)
- white (41)
- tan (43)
- orange (52)
- yellow (57)
- yellow Fr. Knot (57)
- O* white fringe (41)

*Use 2 strands of yarn.

Holly (6 x 4 threads)
(For Sleigh, stitch 2) (For Santa, stitch 2)
(For Reindeer, stitch 4) (For Snowman, stitch 1)
(For Joy, stitch 2) (For Stocking, stitch 2)

Sleigh Package A (5 x 7 threads)

Santa Hat Brim (18 x 4 threads)

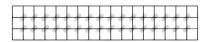

Sleigh Package B (6 x 6 threads)

Sleigh (25 x 19 threads)

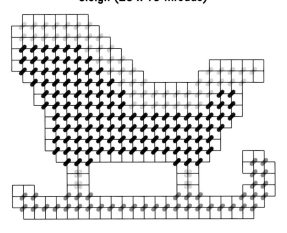

Sleigh Package C (5 x 7 threads)

Santa (17 x 24 threads)

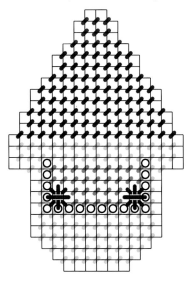

Snowman Hat (15 x 9 threads)

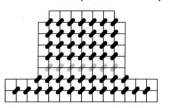

**Reindeer Antler
(13 x 15 threads) (Stitch 2)**

Tree Star (6 x 6 threads)

**Snowman Carrot
(4 x 4 threads)**

Reindeer Face (27 x 11 threads)

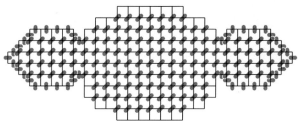

Tree (17 x 22 threads)

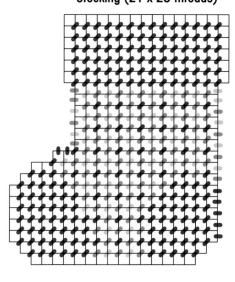

Snowman (9 x 21 threads)

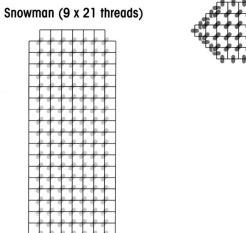

Reindeer Nose (15 x 11 threads)

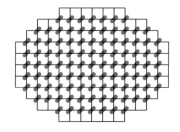

Stocking (21 x 23 threads)

J (12 x 20 threads)

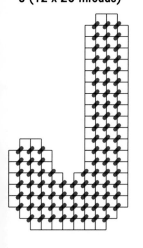

Heart (12 x 10 threads)

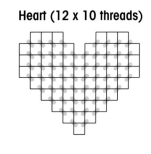

Y (13 x 20 threads)

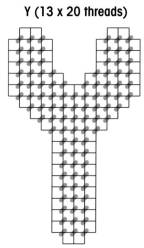

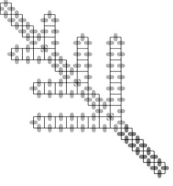

Small Evergreen Branch
(16 x 16 threads) (Stitch 2)

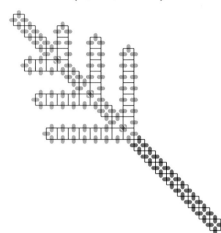

Large Evergreen Branch
(20 x 20 threads)

Snowflake (24 x 24 threads)
Cover edges with white overcast stitches.

COLOR (NL)

- brown (15)
- green (27)
- white (41)

Poinsettia Leaf
(8 x 8 threads) (Stitch 3)

Poinsettia Small Petals
(11 x 11 threads)

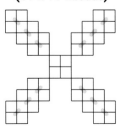

Poinsettia Medium Petals
(13 x 13 threads)

Poinsettia Large Petals
(15 x 15 threads)

Right Eyebrow
(4 x 5 threads)

Left Eyebrow
(4 x 5 threads)

Mustache
(12 x 5 threads)

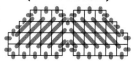

Lovable Santa

Wiggle eyes and a pom-pom nose give this folksy Santa lovable charm. Gold metallic braid adds luster to his beard.

Face (36 x 30 threads)

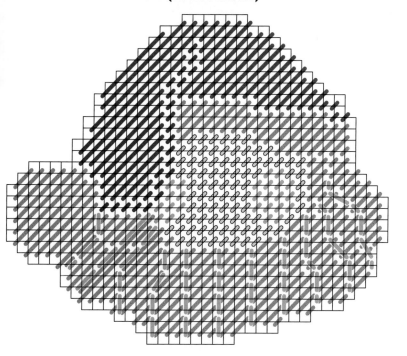

LOVABLE SANTA

Size: 5¼"w x 4½"h

Supplies: Worsted weight yarn, Kreinik metallic gold (002) #16 medium braid, 7 mesh plastic canvas, #16 tapestry needle, two 8mm moving eyes, 7mm pink pom-pom, and clear-drying craft glue

Stitches Used: Backstitch, Gobelin Stitch, Overcast Stitch, and Tent Stitch

Instructions: Follow charts to cut and stitch pieces. Use matching color overcast stitches to cover unworked edges. Glue Mustache, Eyebrows, moving eyes, and pom-pom to Face.

Lovable Santa design by MizFitz.

Classroom Favorites

These teacher-pleasing ornaments are clever accents for dressing up a classroom tree or giving to a favorite instructor. The smart decorations work up so easily, you'll give them an A+!

CLASSROOM FAVORITES

Approx. Size: 3½"w x 3½"h each

Supplies: Worsted weight yarn, 7 mesh plastic canvas, #16 tapestry needle, and clear-drying craft glue

Stitches Used: Backstitch, French Knot, Gobelin Stitch, Lazy Daisy Stitch, Mosaic Stitch, Overcast Stitch, and Tent Stitch

Instructions: Follow charts to cut and stitch pieces for desired ornament. Glue pieces together.

For Bell: If desired, use Numbers chart to add alternate year.

Classroom Favorites designs by Becky Dill.

COLOR (NL)	COLOR (NL)	COLOR
black (00)	green (27)	*black Fr. Knot
red (01)	grey (38)	*red Fr. Knot
lt red (02)	white (41)	*blue Fr. Knot
pink (05)	tan (43)	*green Fr. Knot
lt pink (08)	*white	*white Fr. Knot
yellow (11)	*red	*green Lazy Daisy
brown (14)	*green	*Use 2 plies of yarn.
lt green (25)	red Fr. Knot (01)	

Ruler (32 x 11 threads)

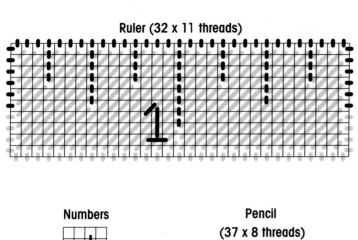

Ruler Santa
(8 x 10 threads)

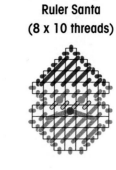

Worm
(7 x 9 threads)

Numbers

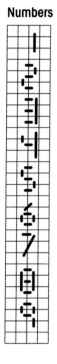

Pencil
(37 x 8 threads)

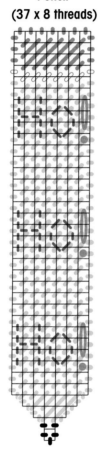
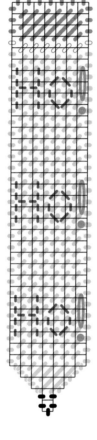

Apple (18 x 18 threads)

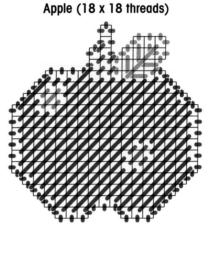

Hat
(7 x 6 threads)

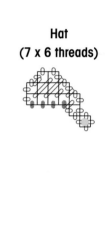

Candy Cane
(5 x 6 threads)
(Stitch 2)

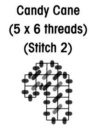

Chalk
(8 x 2 threads)

Chalkboard Santa
(6 x 12 threads)

Bell (19 x 30 threads)

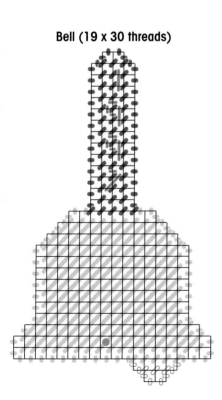

Leaf (6 x 6 threads)
(For Bell, stitch 2)
(For Chalkboard, stitch 2)

Chalkboard (29 x 20 threads)
Complete background before stitching words.

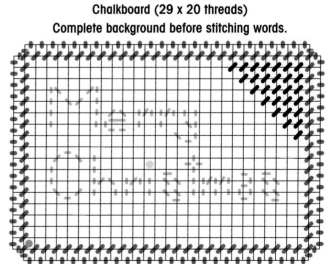

Baby's First Christmas

Baby's first Christmas will be a memorable one with this precious ornament on the tree. The bib-shaped frame holds a wallet-size photo that forever captures a little one's holiday smile

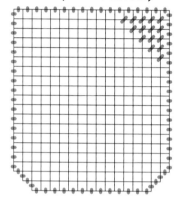

COLOR (NL)

✎	red (02)
✎	green (27)
✎	white (41)

Back (18 x 20 threads)

Front (28 x 38 threads)

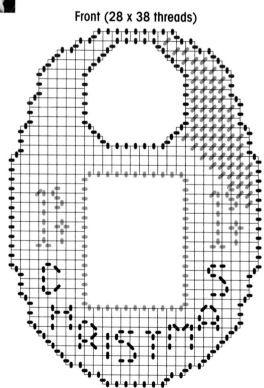

BABY'S FIRST CHRISTMAS

Size: 4¼"w x 5¾"h

(**Note:** Frame opening is approximately 1½"w x 2"h.)

Supplies: Worsted weight yarn, 7 mesh plastic canvas, #16 tapestry needle, 12" of ¼"w red satin ribbon, sewing needle, nylon thread, and clear-drying craft glue

Stitches Used: Backstitch, Overcast Stitch, and Tent Stitch

Instructions: Follow charts to cut and stitch pieces, completing backgrounds with white tent stitches before adding backstitches and overcasting edges. With wrong sides together, center Back over rectangular opening in Front. Leaving top edge open, use sewing needle and nylon thread to tack three sides of Back to Front. Tie ribbon into a bow and glue to Front. Insert desired photo.

Baby's First Christmas design by Virginia Hockenbury.

Holiday Birdhouses

These eye-catching ornaments are for the birds — or, more appropriately, for bird lovers! The quaint collection includes six ornaments that capture the rustic charm of birdhouses.

HOLIDAY BIRDHOUSES

Approx. Size: 3¼"w x 4¾"h each

Supplies: Worsted weight yarn, 7 mesh plastic canvas, #16 tapestry needle, and clear-drying craft glue

Stitches Used: Backstitch, Diagonal Mosaic Stitch, French Knot, Gobelin Stitch, Mosaic Stitch, Overcast Stitch, Scotch Stitch, and Tent Stitch

Instructions: Follow charts and labels to cut and stitch pieces for desired ornament. Glue pieces together.

Holiday Birdhouses designs by Becky Dill.

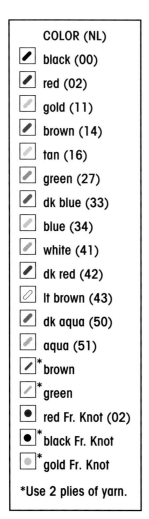

COLOR (NL)

- black (00)
- red (02)
- gold (11)
- brown (14)
- tan (16)
- green (27)
- dk blue (33)
- blue (34)
- white (41)
- dk red (42)
- lt brown (43)
- dk aqua (50)
- aqua (51)
- *brown
- *green
- red Fr. Knot (02)
- *black Fr. Knot
- *gold Fr. Knot

*Use 2 plies of yarn.

Top Flower A
(6 x 6 threads)

Bottom Flower A
(6 x 6 threads)

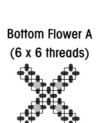

Post B
(4 x 12 threads)

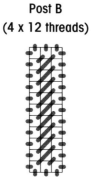

Top Flower B
(9 x 9 threads)

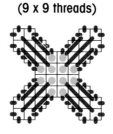

Bottom Flower B
(9 x 9 threads)

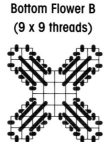

Perch B (15 x 3 threads)

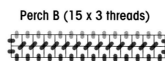

Roof A (20 x 9 threads)

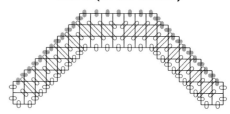

House A (16 x 21 threads)

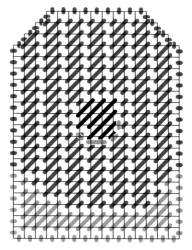

Roof B (22 x 8 threads)

House B (18 x 25 threads)

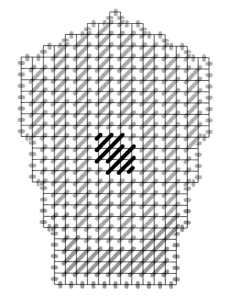

74

House C (18 x 26 threads)

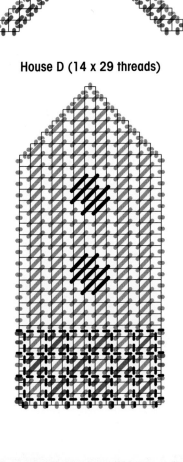

Roof C (12 x 7 threads)

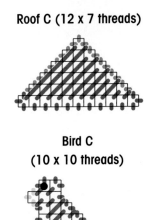

Perch C (20 x 3 threads)

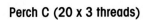

Post C
(4 x 17 threads)

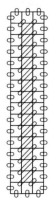

Bird C
(10 x 10 threads)

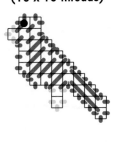

Holly (4 x 4 threads)
(For House C, stitch 2)
(For House D, stitch 3)

Holly F
(6 x 6 threads)
(Stitch 2)

Roof D (18 x 10 threads)

Roof E (20 x 12 threads)

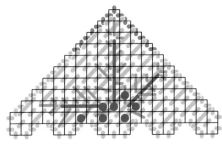

Roof F (18 x 18 threads)

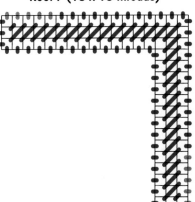

House D (14 x 29 threads)

House E (17 x 26 threads)

House F (15 x 15 threads)

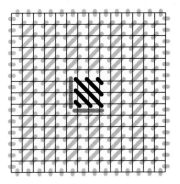

75

Potpourri Cubes

These pretty potpourri-filled ornaments are a breeze to stitch! Airy portions of the white 7 mesh canvas are left unworked, and you can fill the cubes with your favorite fragrance before you join the tops.

POTPOURRI CUBES

Size: 2"w x 2"h x 2"d each

Supplies: Worsted weight yarn, white 7 mesh plastic canvas, #16 tapestry needle, and desired potpourri

Stitches Used: Backstitch, French Knot, Gobelin Stitch, Mosaic Stitch, Overcast Stitch, and Tent Stitch

Instructions: Follow chart to cut and stitch pieces for desired ornament. Join five Sides to form an open cube. Fill cube with potpourri and join sixth Side.

Potpourri Cubes designs by Ann Townsend.

Sides (14 x 14 threads each)
(Stitch 6 matching pieces)

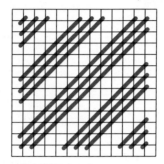
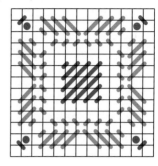

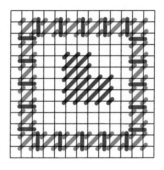
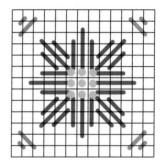

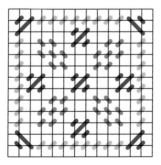
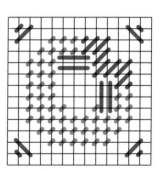

COLOR (NL)

- red (02)
- gold (11)
- green (27)
- red Fr. Knot (02)
- gold Fr. Knot (11)

white (41) - use for joining only

CANDY CANE FRAME

Alternating stitches of red and white create a peppermint pattern on this merry ornament. The heart-shaped frame is a darling way to display a photograph of your little sweetheart.

CANDY CANE FRAME

Size: 3½"w x 3½"h
(**Note:** Frame opening is approximately 2¼"w x 2"h.)
Supplies: Worsted weight yarn, 7 mesh plastic canvas, #16 tapestry needle, three 7mm red pom-poms, and clear-drying craft glue
Stitches Used: Alternating Overcast Stitch, Gobelin Stitch, Overcast Stitch, and Tent Stitch
Instructions: Follow charts to cut and stitch pieces. Position photo behind opening and trim to fit. Use alternating red and white overcast stitches to join Front to Back. Glue Holly and pom-poms to Front.

Candy Cane Frame design by Peggy Astle.

COLOR (NL)	
	red (02)
	green (27)
	white (41)

Holly
(5 x 5 threads)
(Stitch 2)

Front (21 x 21 threads)

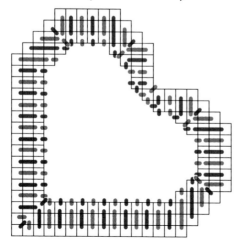

Back (21 x 21 threads)

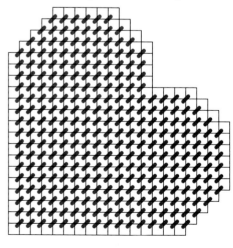

Lacy Treetop Angel

Nothing could be more heavenly than this lacy angel tree topper. The surprisingly simple-to-make Christmas charmer will be ready to take her place atop your tree in no time.

LACY TREETOP ANGEL

Size: 7½"w x 11½"h x 5¼"d

Supplies: Worsted weight yarn, white pearlized metallic yarn, three 10½" x 13½" sheets of 7 mesh plastic canvas, Uniek® 5" plastic canvas star shape, #16 tapestry needle, 78 white 4mm pearl beads, beading needle, and nylon thread

Stitches Used: Backstitch, French Knot, Gobelin Stitch, Overcast Stitch, and Tent Stitch

Instructions: Follow charts to cut pieces, cutting Star from center of Uniek® star shape. Leaving stitches in shaded areas unworked, stitch pieces. Turn Back piece over and work stitches in pink shaded area on wrong side of canvas. Use beading needle and nylon thread to attach beads. Matching ★'s, place right side of Back on wrong side of Body and work stitches in blue shaded area through both thicknesses of canvas to join pieces. Being careful not to carry yarn across slot, match ✖'s and work stitches in pink shaded areas through both thicknesses of canvas to form Angel. Using white overcast stitches, cover unworked edges of Body and Back. Matching ◆'s, place wrong side of Hands on right side of Arms. Work stitches in yellow shaded areas through both thicknesses of canvas to join Hands to Arms. Matching ■'s and ▲'s, tack Arms to Body. Insert tab of Star between Hands and Arms. Insert tab of Wings into slot in back of Body.

Lacy Treetop Angel design by Dick Martin.

COLOR (NL)

- ✐ pink (07) - 1yd
- ✐ white (41) - 60 yds
- ✐ tan (43) - 8 yds
- ✐ flesh (56) - 3 yds
- ✐* dk pink - 1 yd
- ● black Fr. Knot (00) - 1 yd
- ✐ pearlized metallic - 3 yds
- ● bead
- ✐ cutting line

*Use 2 plies of yarn.

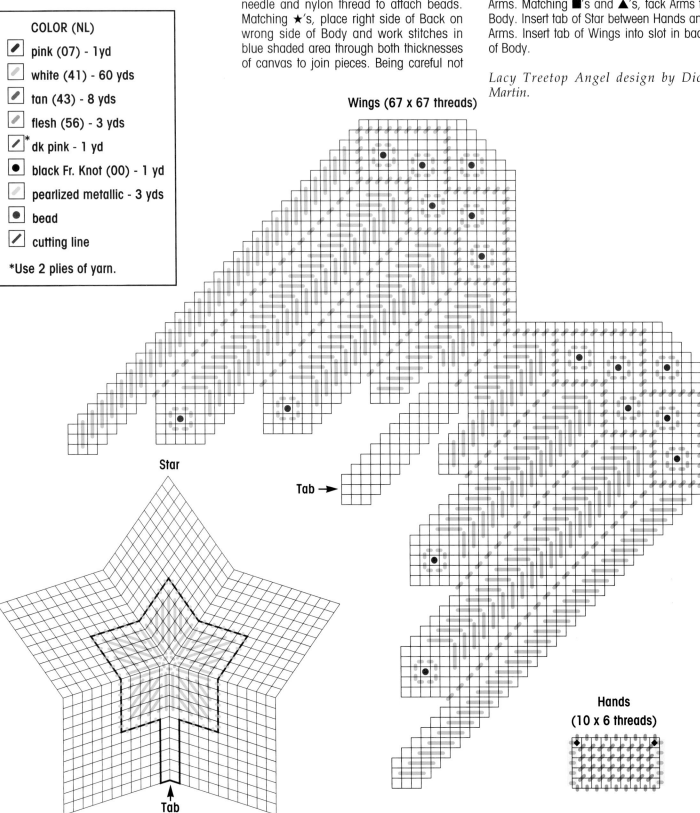

Wings (67 x 67 threads)

Star

Tab →

Tab

Hands (10 x 6 threads)

Arms (70 x 6 threads)

Body (71 x 71 threads)

Slot

Back (25 x 25 threads)

Slot

Festive Pets

These doggone cute ornaments are the cat's meow! Worked on 7 mesh plastic canvas, the adorable critters get their lovable expressions from wiggle eyes and pom-pom noses. Red ribbon bow-ties and holly give them a festive finish.

FESTIVE PETS

Dog Size: 3¼"w x 4"h

Dog Supplies: Worsted weight yarn, 7 mesh plastic canvas, #16 tapestry needle, two 6mm moving eyes, three 7mm red pom-poms, 7mm black pom-pom, 8" of ¼"w red satin ribbon, and clear-drying craft glue

Stitches Used: Cross Stitch, Overcast Stitch, and Tent Stitch

Dog Instructions: Follow charts to cut and stitch pieces. Cover unworked edges of Ears with brown overcast stitches. Cover remaining unworked edges with tan overcast stitches. Glue pieces together. Glue pom-poms and ribbon bow to Dog.

Cat Size: 3¼"w x 4¼"h

Cat Supplies: Worsted weight yarn, 7 mesh plastic canvas, #16 tapestry needle, two 6mm moving eyes, three 7mm red pom-poms, 7mm black pom-pom, 8" of ¼"w red satin ribbon, 6" of black cloth-covered wire, and clear-drying craft glue

Stitches Used: Backstitch, Cross Stitch, Overcast Stitch, and Tent Stitch

Cat Instructions: Follow charts to cut and stitch pieces. Before working grey backstitches on Arms, cover all unworked edges with lt grey overcast stitches. Glue pieces together. Referring to photo, bend and trim wire for mouth. Glue wire, pom-poms, and ribbon bow to Cat.

Festive Pets designs by Studio M.

COLOR (NL)	
✎	brown (15)
✎	green (27)
✎	lt grey (37)
✎	grey (38)
✎	tan (43)
✎*	grey

*Use 2 plies of yarn.

Dog Right Ear (8 x 9 threads)

Dog Left Ear (8 x 9 threads)
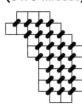

Dog Nose (5 x 5 threads)

Holly (4 x 6 threads)
(For Cat, stitch 2)
(For Dog, stitch 2)

Cat Right Arm (11 x 5 threads)
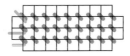

Dog (8 x 20 threads)
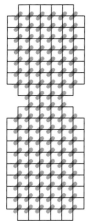
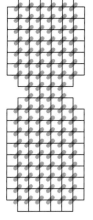

Cat (10 x 22 threads)
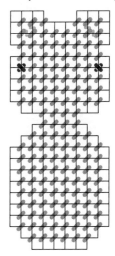

Cat Left Arm (11 x 5 threads)

Dog Right Arm (11 x 5 threads)
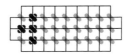

Dog Right Leg (7 x 11 threads)
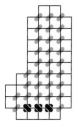

Dog Left Leg (7 x 11 threads)
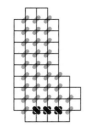

Dog Left Arm (11 x 5 threads)
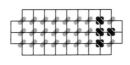

Cat Right Leg (7 x 11 threads)

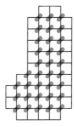

Cat Left Leg (7 x 11 threads)
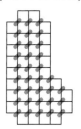

Mood Messages

The contrasting messages on this witty ornament offer a fun way to advertise your Christmas mood. When you feel like celebrating, display the "Joy" sign. And when the holiday bustle gets to be too much, flip it over to "Bah! Humbug!"

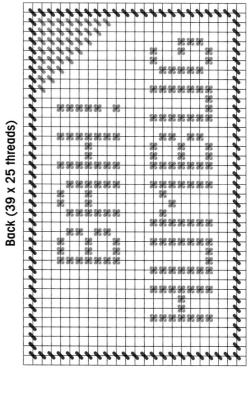

Back (39 x 25 threads)

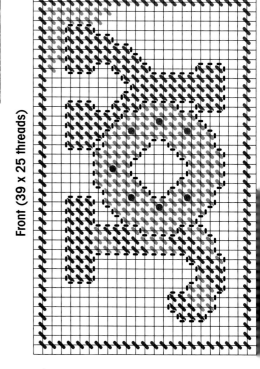

Front (39 x 25 threads)

MOOD MESSAGES

Size: 5³/₄"w x 3³/₄"h

Supplies: Worsted weight yarn, 7 mesh plastic canvas, #16 tapestry needle, 22" of ¹/₄"w red satin ribbon, sewing needle, and thread

Stitches Used: Backstitch, Cross Stitch, French Knot, Overcast Stitch, and Tent Stitch

Instructions: Follow charts to cut and stitch pieces. Before adding backstitch, complete backgrounds with white tent stitches. Cut an 8" piece from ribbon and tie into a bow. Use sewing needle and thread to tack bow to Front. Tack ends of remaining ribbon to wrong side of Front for hanger. Join Front to Back.

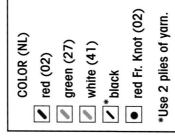

COLOR (NL)	
✏	red (02)
✏	green (27)
✏	white (41)
✏	* black
●	red Fr. Knot (02)
*Use 2 plies of yarn.	

North Pole Trio

This North Pole trio will greet guests with a cheery holiday welcome! Stitched over clear and tan 7 mesh plastic canvas, the three-dimensional characters can be hung on your tree or arranged on a tabletop for a spirited display.

NORTH POLE TRIO

Supplies: Worsted weight yarn, clear 7 mesh plastic canvas, #16 tapestry needle, and clear nylon thread

Additional Reindeer Supply: Tan 7 mesh plastic canvas

Stitches Used: Backstitch, Cross Stitch, French Knot, Gobelin Stitch, Overcast Stitch, Tent Stitch, and Turkey Loop Stitch

Santa Size: 5¾"w x 7"h x 2"d

Santa Instructions: Follow charts to cut pieces from clear canvas. Leaving stitches in shaded areas unworked, stitch pieces. Turn Hat over and stitch shaded area on wrong side. Match ✖'s and tack wrong side of Arms to wrong side of Back. With right side of Hat facing up, match ★'s and place Hat between Front and Back. Join Front to Back along unworked edges, stitching through all thicknesses at Hat. Tack Buckle to unworked thread at center of Coat. Match ▲'s and work stitches in shaded area to join ends of Coat, forming a cylinder. Join unworked edge of Coat Trim to bottom edge of Coat. Tack ends of Coat Trim together. Slide Coat over Santa, allowing Arms to fit into slots. Thread two 12" strands of clear nylon thread through top sections of Coat. Pull ends of thread to gather Coat around neck and tie securely. Join bottom edges of Front and Back to stitched Base along unworked threads between black and white stitched areas. Join unstitched Base to wrong side of stitched Base. Bend Hat tip backwards so that Turkey Loop pom-pom is facing forward. Tack pom-pom to band of Hat. Tack thumb of Right Arm to band of Hat.

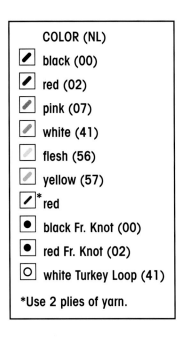

COLOR (NL)	
▨	black (00)
▨	red (02)
▨	pink (07)
▨	white (41)
▨	flesh (56)
▨	yellow (57)
▨*	red
●	black Fr. Knot (00)
●	red Fr. Knot (02)
◉	white Turkey Loop (41)

*Use 2 plies of yarn.

Right Arm (8 x 18 threads)

Left Arm (8 x 18 threads)

Coat (36 x 33 threads)

slot

slot

Coat Trim (30 x 30 threads)

Santa Front (37 x 37 threads)

Base (20 x 20 threads)
(Cut 2, Stitch 1)

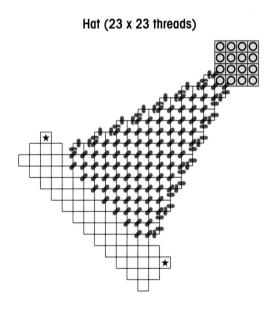

Buckle (5 x 5 threads)

Hat (23 x 23 threads)

Santa Back (37 x 37 threads)

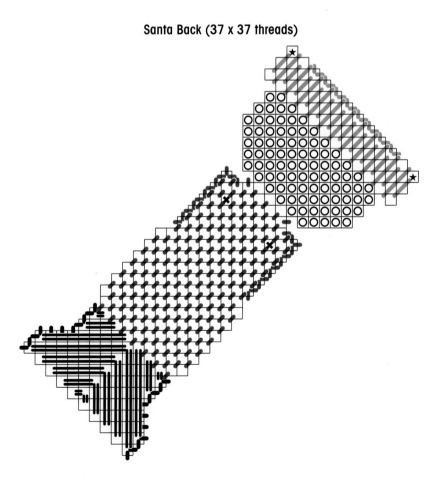

Reindeer Size: 5"w x 4¹/₂"h

Reindeer Instructions: Follow charts to cut and stitch Side A and Side B pieces on tan canvas. Cut and stitch Wreath on clear canvas. Join Side A to Side B along unworked edges. Place Wreath around Reindeer's neck. Thread 12" of red yarn through ends of Wreath and tie yarn into a bow. Refer to photo and the following instructions to add harness. Leaving last 6" of yarn free for rein, thread 12" of an 18" length of red yarn from Side A to Side B at ▲'s. Insert needle again at ▲'s from Side A to Side B to make stitch across nose. Insert needle again at ▲'s from Side A to Side B and loop stitch between ears and antlers. Tie loose ends of yarn together for reins and trim.

Mrs. Claus Size: 3"w x 6¹/₂"h x 2³/₄"d

Mrs. Claus Instructions: Follow charts to cut pieces from clear canvas. Leaving shaded areas unworked, stitch pieces. Join Front to Back. Match ■'s and stitch shaded areas to join Bonnet pieces. Slip Bonnet over top of Mrs. Claus and tack in place. Match ★'s and complete stitches in shaded area to join ends of Dress, forming a cylinder. Slide Dress over Mrs. Claus, allowing arms to fit into slots of Dress. Thread two 12" strands of clear nylon thread through top sections of Dress. Pull ends of thread to gather top of Dress around neck and tie securely. Join Plum Pudding pieces. Make two green Turkey Loop Stitches on top of Plum Pudding. Match ✱'s and tack Plum Pudding to Tray. Tack Tray to hands.

North Pole Trio designs by Dick Martin.

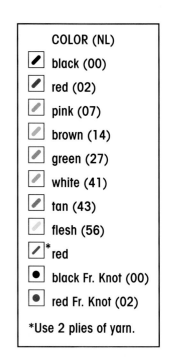

COLOR (NL)	
✎	black (00)
✎	red (02)
✎	pink (07)
✎	brown (14)
✎	green (27)
✎	white (41)
✎	tan (43)
▢	flesh (56)
✎	*red
●	black Fr. Knot (00)
●	red Fr. Knot (02)
*Use 2 plies of yarn.	

Reindeer Side A (30 x 41 threads)

Reindeer Side B (30 x 41 threads)

Wreath (12 x 12 threads)

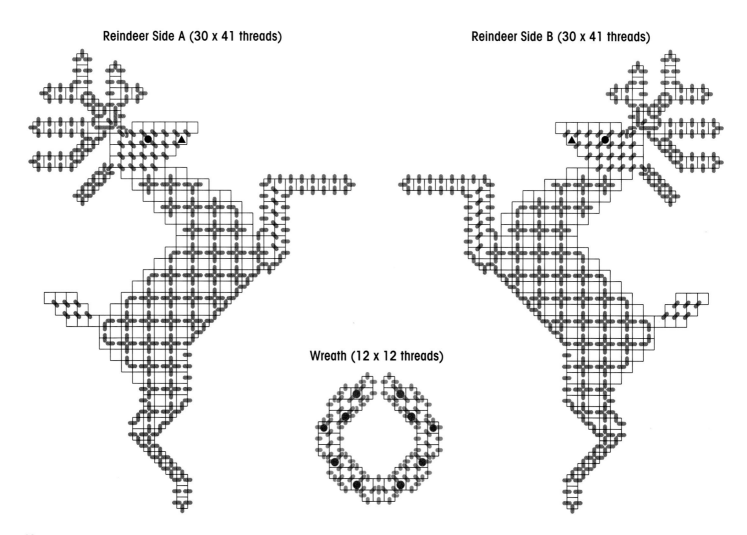

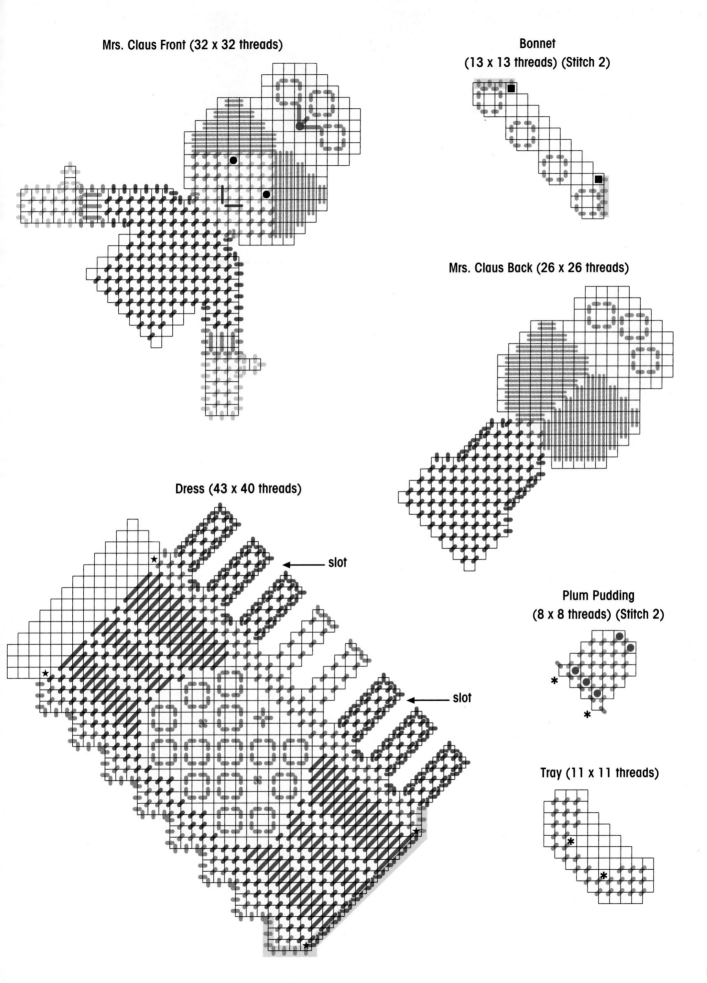

Mrs. Claus Front (32 x 32 threads)

Bonnet
(13 x 13 threads) (Stitch 2)

Mrs. Claus Back (26 x 26 threads)

Dress (43 x 40 threads)

slot

slot

Plum Pudding
(8 x 8 threads) (Stitch 2)

Tray (11 x 11 threads)

89

Santa Star

Santa makes a "star" appearance in this simple ornament that's perfect for beginners. His body takes shape from a precut form, and his jovial expression is crafted with wiggle eyes, a French-knot nose, and a pom-pom beard.

Hat

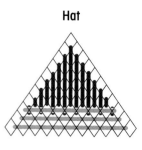

Left Boot
(10 x 8 threads)

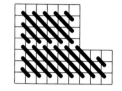

Right Boot
(10 x 8 threads)

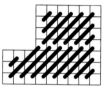

SANTA STAR

Size: 5¹/₂"w x 6"h

Supplies: Worsted weight yarn, 7 mesh plastic canvas, two Uniek® 5" plastic canvas star shapes, #16 tapestry needle, nine ¹/₂" white pom-poms, two 6mm moving eyes, and clear-drying craft glue

Stitches Used: Backstitch, French Knot, Gobelin Stitch, and Overcast Stitch

Instructions: Follow charts to cut Hat from point of one star shape and Boots from 7 mesh canvas. Stitch pieces. Use matching color overcast stitches to cover unworked edges. Glue Boots, Hat, moving eyes, and pom-poms to Santa.

Santa Star design by Ann Townsend.

Santa

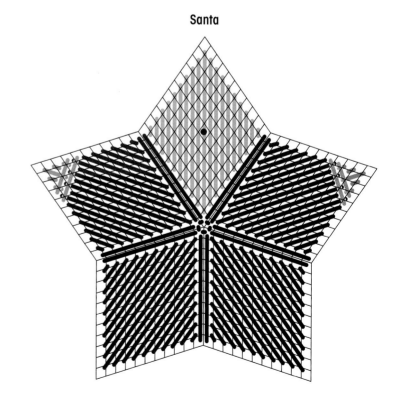

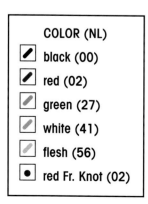

COLOR (NL)
- black (00)
- red (02)
- green (27)
- white (41)
- flesh (56)
- • red Fr. Knot (02)

Teddy Poinsettia

Let's face it, this teddy poinsettia is adorable! To make the blooming bear, just stitch him on 7 mesh plastic canvas and glue him to the center of a silk poinsettia. He'll make a "beary" festive ornament for your tree.

TEDDY POINSETTIA

Size: 2"w x 2"h

Supplies: Worsted weight yarn, 7 mesh plastic canvas, #16 tapestry needle, two 7mm moving eyes, 6" silk poinsettia, and clear-drying craft glue

Stitches Used: Backstitch, Gobelin Stitch, Overcast Stitch, and Tent Stitch

Instructions: Follow charts to cut and stitch pieces. Glue Nose and moving eyes to Teddy. Glue Teddy to center of poinsettia.

Teddy Poinsettia design by Linda Huffman.

COLOR (NL)	
/	pink (08)
/	tan (40)
/	brown (43)
/	*black

***Use 2 plies of yarn.**

Teddy (14 x 13 threads)

Nose (8 x 5 threads)

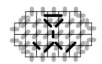

GENERAL INSTRUCTIONS

READING THE CHART

Whenever possible, the drawing on the chart looks like the completed stitch. For example, a tent stitch on the chart is drawn diagonally across one intersection of threads just like a tent stitch looks when stitched on your canvas. A symbol will be used on the chart when a stitch, such as a French knot, cannot be clearly drawn. If you have difficulty determining how a particular stitch should be worked, refer to the list of stitches in the project information and the stitch diagrams on pages 94-96.

Overcast stitches have been omitted from the charts, when possible, in order to make the cutting line easy to follow. When overcast stitches are omitted from the chart, the project instructions or a note above the chart will tell you the color overcast stitches to use.

When backstitches used for detail, French knots, and lazy daisy stitches appear on a chart, remember to complete background stitches before working these stitches.

READING THE COLOR KEY

A color key is given with each chart. The key indicates the color yarn, floss, or braid to use for each stitch on the chart. All straight stitches are represented by a line of color in the color key. For example, when white yarn is represented by a grey line in the color key, all grey stitches on the chart should be stitched using white yarn. When a stitch is represented by a symbol on the chart, the same symbol will be used in the color key to tell you the stitch and color to use.

To help you select colors for your project, we have included color numbers for Needloft® Plastic Canvas Yarn (NL), DMC Embroidery Floss (DMC), and Kreinik Metallic Braid (KREINIK) in some color keys. Many brands of yarn, embroidery floss, and braid are available and may be used to stitch your project.

Additional information may also be included in the color key, such as the number of strands or plies to use when working a particular stitch.

SELECTING PLASTIC CANVAS

Plastic canvas is a molded material that consists of "threads" and "holes." The threads aren't actually "threads" since the canvas is not woven, but it seems to be a good description of the straight lines of the canvas. Project instructions often refer to the threads, especially when cutting out plastic canvas pieces. The holes, as you would expect, are the spaces between the threads. The stitch diagrams, pages 94-96, will refer to holes when explaining where to place your needle to make a stitch.

TYPES OF CANVAS

The main difference between types of plastic canvas is the mesh size. Mesh size refers to the number of threads in one inch of canvas. The projects in this book were stitched using 7 mesh, 10 mesh, or 14 mesh canvas. Seven mesh means that there are 7 threads in every inch of canvas. Likewise, 10 threads in every inch of 10 mesh canvas, and 14 threads in every inch of 14 mesh canvas. Seven mesh canvas is the most popular size for projects.

The project supply list will tell you the size mesh canvas needed for your project. If a project calls for 7 mesh canvas and you use 10 mesh, your finished project will be much smaller than expected.

Most projects in this book are stitched on clear canvas. A few projects are stitched on colored canvas or specialty plastic canvas shapes. These items should be available at your local craft store.

AMOUNT OF CANVAS

For large projects, such as tree toppers, the project supply list will tell you how much canvas will be needed to complete the project. As a general rule, it is better to buy too much canvas and have leftovers than to run out of canvas before you finish your project. Since scraps of canvas are excellent for making the small projects in this book, we have not specified an amount of canvas in most project supply lists. One sheet of plastic canvas will be enough to make several small items.

SELECTING NEEDLES

TYPES OF NEEDLES

A blunt needle called a tapestry needle is used for stitching on plastic canvas. Tapestry needles are sized by numbers; the higher the number, the smaller the needle. The correct size needle to use depends on the canvas mesh size and the yarn thickness. The needle should be small enough to allow the threaded needle to pass through the canvas holes easily. The eye of the needle should be large enough to allow yarn to be threaded easily. If the eye is too small, the yarn will wear thin and may break. You will find the recommended needle size listed in the supply section of each project. The chart below will be helpful when selecting the correct needle for your project.

Mesh	Needle
7	#16 tapestry
10	#20 tapestry
14	#24 tapestry

SELECTING YARN

We have a few hints to help you choose the perfect yarns for your project and your budget.

COLORS

The project color key will tell you the color yarn needed to stitch your project. Brand names and color numbers listed in some color keys are included only as a guide when choosing colors for your project.

Remember, you don't have to use the colors suggested in the color key. If you find a green and gold ornament that you really like, but you plan to decorate your tree with red and silver, simply substitute the colors you prefer.

TYPES OF YARN

The types of yarns available are almost endless, and each grouping of yarn has its own characteristics and uses. The following is a brief description of some common yarns used for plastic canvas.

Worsted Weight Yarn - Worsted weight yarn is the most popular yarn used for 7 mesh plastic canvas because one strand covers the canvas well. This yarn may be found in acrylic, wool, wool blends, and a variety of other fiber contents. Acrylic yarn is a favorite because it is reasonably priced and comes in a wide variety of colors. Most brands of worsted weight yarn have four plies that are twisted together to form one strand. When the instructions indicate 2 plies of yarn, you will need to separate a strand of yarn into its plies and use only the number of plies indicated in the instructions.

Needloft® Yarn is a 100% nylon worsted weight yarn and is suitable only for 7 mesh plastic canvas. It will not easily separate. When stitching with Needloft® Yarn and the instructions indicate 2 plies of yarn, we recommend that you substitute 6 strands of embroidery floss.

Sport Weight Yarn - Sport weight yarn works nicely for 10 mesh canvas. This yarn has three or four thin plies that are twisted together to form one strand. Like worsted weight yarn, sport weight yarn comes in a variety of fiber contents. The color selection in sport weight yarn is more limited than in other types of yarns.

FLOSS AND METALLICS

Embroidery Floss - Embroidery floss is made up of six strands. For smooth coverage when using embroidery floss, separate and realign the strands of floss before threading your needle. Twelve strands of floss may be used for covering 10 mesh canvas. Use six strands to cover 14 mesh canvas. Occasionally, embroidery floss is used to add details on 7 mesh canvas.

Metallic Yarn - This flat yarn is soft, flexible, and durable. Metallic yarn can be used to add decorative details to a project or for general coverage. It is available in different sizes for use with various mesh sizes. Use 18" or shorter lengths of metallic yarn for easier stitching and to avoid fraying. Since metallic yarn is flat instead of round like other yarns and metallic braids, care must be used to make sure the yarn lies flat when stitched on the canvas.

Metallic Braid - Metallic braid is available in a variety of sizes and may be used to add finishing details to a project or for general coverage. Using 18" or shorter lengths of metallic braid will make stitching easier and avoid excessive wear.

WORKING WITH PLASTIC CANVAS

Throughout this book, the lines of the canvas will be referred to as threads. To cut plastic canvas pieces accurately, count **threads** (not **holes**) as shown in **Fig. 1**. If you accidentally count holes, your piece will be the wrong size.

Fig. 1

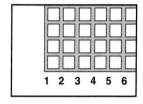

PREPARING AND CUTTING CANVAS
Before cutting out your pieces, note the thread count located above the chart for each piece. The thread count tells you the number of threads in the width and the height of the canvas piece. Follow the thread count to cut a rectangle the specified size. Remembering to count **threads**, not **holes**, follow the chart to trim the rectangle into the desired shape.

You may want to use an overhead projector pen to outline the piece on the canvas before cutting it out. Before you begin stitching, be sure to remove all markings with a damp towel. Any remaining markings could rub off on the yarn as you stitch.

A good pair of household scissors is recommended for cutting plastic canvas. However, a craft knife is helpful when cutting in small areas. When using a craft knife, make sure to protect the table below your canvas with a layer of cardboard or a magazine.

When cutting canvas, be sure to cut as close to the thread as possible without cutting into the thread. If you don't cut close enough, "nubs" or "pickets" will be left on the edge of your canvas. Be sure to cut off all nubs from the canvas before you begin to stitch, because nubs will snag the yarn and are difficult to cover.

When cutting plastic canvas along a diagonal, cut through the center of each intersection **(Fig. 2)**. This will leave enough plastic canvas on both sides of the cut so that both pieces of canvas may be used. Properly cut diagonal corners will be less likely to snag yarn and are easier to cover.

Fig. 2

THREADING YOUR NEEDLE
Here are a couple of methods that may make threading your needle easier. Several brands of yarn-size needle threaders are available at your local craft store.

FOLD METHOD
First, sharply fold the end of yarn over your needle; then remove needle. Keeping the fold sharp, push the needle onto the yarn **(Fig. 3)**.

Fig. 3

THREAD METHOD
Fold a 5" piece of sewing thread in half, forming a loop. Insert loop of thread through the eye of your needle **(Fig. 4)**. Insert yarn through the loop and pull the thread back through your needle, pulling yarn through at the same time.

Fig. 4

STITCH DIAGRAMS

Unless otherwise indicated, bring threaded needle up at 1 and all odd numbers and down at 2 and all even numbers.

ALTERNATING OVERCAST STITCH

This stitch covers the edge of the canvas and joins pieces of canvas. With first color, work overcast stitches in every other hole. Then with second color, work overcast stitches in the remaining holes (Fig. 5).

Fig. 5

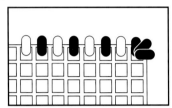

BACKSTITCH

This stitch is worked over completed stitches to outline or define (Fig. 6). It is sometimes worked over more than one thread. Backstitch may also be used to cover canvas as shown in Fig. 7.

Fig. 6

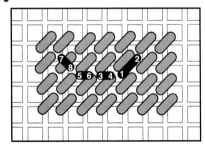

Fig. 7

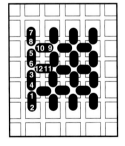

CROSS STITCH

This stitch is composed of two stitches (Fig. 8). The top stitch of each cross must always be made in the same direction. The number of intersections covered may vary according to the chart.

Fig. 8

DIAGONAL MOSAIC STITCH

This stitch is a variation of the mosaic stitch. It is worked in diagonal rows as shown in Fig. 9.

Fig. 9

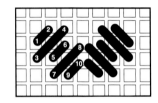

DOUBLE CROSS STITCH

This stitch is composed of four stitches (Fig. 10). The top stitch of each cross must always be made in the same direction. Follow Fig. 11 to work the Reversed Double Cross Stitch.

Fig. 10

Fig. 11

FRENCH KNOT

Bring needle up through hole. Wrap yarn once around needle and insert needle in same hole or adjacent hole, holding yarn with non-stitching fingers (Fig. 12). Tighten knot; then pull needle through canvas, holding yarn until it must be released.

Fig. 12

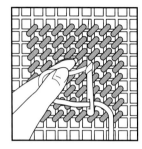

FRINGE STITCH

Fold a 12" length of yarn in half. Thread needle with loose ends of yarn. Take needle down at 1, leaving a loop on top of the canvas. Come up at 2, bring needle through loop, and pull tightly (Fig. 13). Trim fringe to desired length.

Fig. 13

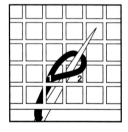

GOBELIN STITCH

This basic straight stitch is worked over two or more threads or intersections. The number of threads or intersections may vary according to the chart (Fig. 14).

Fig. 14

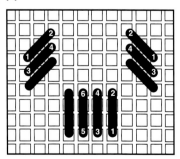

LAZY DAISY STITCH

Bring needle up at 1; make a loop and go down at 1 again **(Fig. 15)**. Come up at 2, keeping yarn below needle's point. Pull yarn through and secure loop by bringing yarn over loop and going down at 2.

Fig. 15

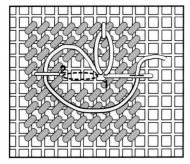

MOSAIC STITCH

This three-stitch pattern forms small squares **(Fig. 16)**.

Fig. 16

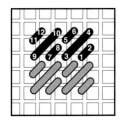

OVERCAST STITCH

This stitch is used to cover the edge of the canvas or to join pieces of canvas **(Fig. 17)**. When using overcast stitches to cover an edge, it may be necessary to go through the same hole more than once to get even coverage. When turning corners, make one stitch into inside corners and three stitches to cover an outside corner.

Fig. 17

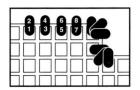

SCOTCH STITCH

This stitch forms a square. It may be worked over three or more horizontal threads by three or more vertical threads. **Fig. 18** shows it worked over three threads.

Fig. 18

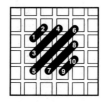

SMYRNA CROSS STITCH

This stitch is worked over two threads as a decorative stitch. Each stitch is worked completely before going on to the next **(Fig. 19)**.

Fig. 19

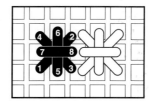

TENT STITCH

This stitch is worked in horizontal or vertical rows over one intersection as shown in **Fig. 20**. Follow **Fig. 21** to work the **Reversed Tent Stitch**.

Fig. 20

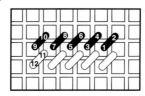

Fig. 21

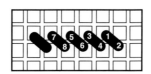

Sometimes when you are working Tent Stitches, the last stitch on the row will look "pulled" on the front of your piece when you are changing directions. To avoid this problem, leave a loop of yarn on the wrong side of the stitched piece after making the last stitch in the row. When making the first stitch in the next row, run your needle through the loop **(Fig. 22)**. Gently pull yarn until all stitches are even.

Fig. 22

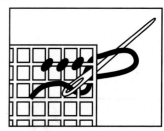

TURKEY LOOP STITCH

This stitch is composed of locked loops. Bring needle up through hole and back down through same hole, forming a loop on top of the canvas. A locking stitch is then made across the thread directly below or to either side of loop as shown in **Fig. 23**.

Fig. 23

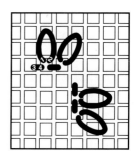

TURKEY LOOP VARIATION STITCH

This stitch is composed of locked loops. Bring needle up through hole and back down through next hole, forming a loop on top of the canvas. A locking stitch is then made by bringing needle up and down in same holes as shown in **Fig. 24**. Clip the loop to form fringe. Trim to desired length and separate plies.

Fig. 24

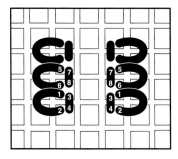

UPRIGHT CROSS STITCH

This stitch is worked over two threads as shown in **Fig. 25**. The top stitch of each cross must always be made in the same direction.

Fig. 25

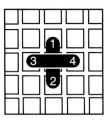

TACKING AND JOINING

Tacking and joining are methods used to assemble stitched pieces.

Tacking is used when you want to securely attach two pieces without the stitches being seen. To tack, follow the project instructions for placement and use several small stitches to attach the pieces together.

Joining stitched pieces is usually done with overcast stitches. Use matching color overcast stitches for joining, unless otherwise indicated. Stitch through holes as many times as necessary to completely cover the canvas.

Join pieces with straight edges by carefully aligning edges and stitching through all layers. When joining pieces with uneven edges, the holes will not line up exactly. Just keep the pieces as even as possible.

When joining the edge of one piece to an area of unworked threads of another piece, match the indicated threads or symbols and stitch through all layers.

Shaded areas often mean that the stitches in that area are used to join pieces of canvas. The project instructions will tell you when to complete shaded areas.

MAKING A YARN TWIST

Refer to the project instructions for the color and finished length of the yarn twist. Multiply finished length of twist by two. This is the length you will need to cut each strand of yarn used to make the twist. Cut two strands of yarn the required length. Place strands of yarn together and tie a knot at one end. With one loose end in each hand, pull yarn taut. While holding one end stationary, keep yarn taut and twist yarn in a clockwise motion until tight. Keeping yarn taut, fold yarn in half at knot to bring loose ends together. Release yarn at knot; yarn will twist together. Knot loose ends at desired length and trim ends. Pull yarn twist through fingers to evenly distribute twist.

MAKING A HANGER

Thread 8" of nylon thread or ribbon through top of the ornament. Knot ends together 3" above ornament and trim ends.

WASHING INSTRUCTIONS

If you used washable yarn for all of your stitches, you may hand wash plastic canvas projects in warm water with a mild soap. Do not rub or scrub stitches; this will cause the yarn to fuzz. Allow your stitched piece to air dry. Do not put stitched pieces in a clothes dryer. The plastic canvas could melt in the heat of a dryer. Do not dry clean your plastic canvas. The chemicals used in dry cleaning could dissolve the plastic canvas. When piece is dry, you may need to trim the fuzz from your project with a small pair of sharp scissors.

Instructions tested and photography items made by Kandi Ashford, Toni Bowden, Virginia Cates, Wanda Hopkins, Connie McGauhey, Sadie Wilson, and Janie Wright.